PEBBLES FROM THE BROOK

*Sermons for Children Who are
Fighting the Good Fight of Faith*

RICHARD NEWTON

SOLID GROUND CHRISTIAN BOOKS
Birmingham, Alabama USA
February 2011

Other Related Titles for Children

In addition to *Pebbles from the Brook* we are delighted to offer several other titles from Solid Ground Christian Books for the young. Here is a sample:

Little Pillows and Morning Bells by Miss Havergal
Morning Stars by Miss Havergal
The Child's Book on the Fall by Thomas H Gallaudet
The Child's Book on the Soul by T.H. Gallaudet
The Child's Book of Natural Theology by Gallaudet
The Child's Book on the Sabbath by Horace Hooker
Feed My Lambs by John Todd
Truth Made Simple by John Todd
The Tract Primer by the American Tract Society
The Child at Home by John S.C. Abbott
Early Piety Illustrated by Gorham Abbott
Repentance & Faith for the Young by Charles Walker
Jesus the Way by Edward Payson Hammond
The Pastor's Daughter by Louisa Payson Hopkins
Lectures on the Bible to the Young by John Eadie
The Scripture Guide by James W. Alexander
My Brother's Keeper by James W. Alexander
The Chief End of Man by John Hall
Old Paths for Little Feet by Carol Brandt
Small Talks on Big Questions by Selah Helms
Advice to a Young Christian by Jared Waterbury
Bible Promises by Richard Newton
Bible Warnings by Richard Newton
Bible Models by Richard Newton
Bible Animals by Richard Newton
Bible Jewels by Richard Newton
Heroes of the Early Church by Richard Newton
Heroes of the Reformation by Richard Newton
Safe Compass and How it Points by Richard Newton
The King's Highway by Richard Newton
The Life of Jesus Christ for the Young by Richard Newton
Rays from the Sun of Righteousness by Richard Newton

Call us at **1-205-443-0311**
Visit us on-line at www.solid-ground-books.com

PEBBLES

FROM THE BROOK.

Sermons to Children.

BY THE

REV. RICHARD NEWTON, D.D.,

AUTHOR OF THE "JEWEL CASE," "WONDER CASE," ETC.

———◆◆———

NEW YORK:

ROBERT CARTER AND BROTHERS,

530 BROADWAY.

1880.

Solid Ground Christian Books
PO Box 660132
Vestavia Hills AL 35266
205-443-0311
sgcb@charter.net
www.solid-ground-books.com

PEBBLES FROM THE BROOK
Sermons to Children Fighting the Good Fight of Faith

by Richard Newton (1813-1887)

Taken from the 1880 edition by *Robert Carter & Brothers*, NY

Cover image is taken from a photo by Ric Ergenbright
Wet pebbles, Glacier National Park, Montana.

Cover design by Borgo Design
Contact them at borgogirl@bellsouth.net

ISBN- 978-159925-151-6

PREFACE.

THE title of this book carries back our minds to David, the shepherd boy of Bethlehem. We think of him as sent by his father to visit his brothers, who were soldiers in the army of Israel. He finds the whole army trembling with fear, as the Philistine giant challenges any among them to engage in single combat with him. We think of David's surprise when he finds no one willing to take up the challenge, and fight that boasting Philistine, who is proudly defying the army of the living God.

We remember how bravely that youthful stripling offers to go and do what all Saul's heroes are afraid to do. We see him arrayed in Saul's armor. But he cannot go in this. He puts it off. He takes his sling with him. He chooses five smooth stones from the brook. Thus armed, he goes against the giant. By the help of God, with one of those pebbles, he hurls the giant to the earth, and gains a glorious victory over him.

We all have giants to fight. Every form of sin is such a giant. We can only succeed in this warfare by following David's example. The brook, to which we must go for our pebbles, is the word of God. Every portion of truth from this word is a pebble for our use in this warfare. When Jesus, the Captain of our salvation, went forth into the wilderness, to be tempted of Satan, he was fighting the great father of all the giants. He fought and conquered him with pebbles from this brook. And if we seek the help of God, to enable us to use these pebbles, as our blessed master did, we shall be successful as he was.

And if the pebbles here chosen from this brook, shall prove useful to any young persons, in their conflict with the giant evils around them, the aim of the author in sending forth this little volume will be secured.

R. N.

November, 1879.

CONTENTS.

I.

THE BEST CAPTAIN.

I.

THE BEST CAPTAIN.

" The Captain of their salvation." — Hebrews ii. 10.

We read a good deal about soldiers in the Bible. The church of Jesus Christ is compared to an army. When Solomon is speaking of this church, he represents it as marching on its way like " an army with banners." And Christian people are compared to soldiers. The apostle Paul says that those who wish to be the true servants of Christ must learn to "endure hardness as good soldiers of Jesus Christ." And in another place he tells them how they are to "put on the whole armor of God," taking the helmet, and the breastplate, and the shield, and the girdle, and the sword, as every soldier had to do in those days.

And then, in the words we have taken for our present text, Jesus is spoken of as the Captain of salvation to his people, the Head and

Leader of this great army. And there is one place in the Old Testament where Jesus speaks of himself as the Captain of his people. This was after the Israelites had crossed over the river Jordan, and were going to make an attack on the city of Jericho. The army of the Israelites was encamped outside the walls of the city, and Joshua, their leader, was getting ready to make an attack upon the city ; when, one day, Jesus came to him in the appearance of a soldier, with a drawn sword in his hand. He told Joshua that he was the Captain of his people, and had come to tell him what he was to do.

And so now, we are to speak of Jesus as " the Captain of our salvation." It is very important for soldiers to have a good captain. They never can expect to get the victory over their enemies without this. We read in history of many famous captains. Alexander the Great was one of these. And so was Julius Cæsar, and Napoleon Bonaparte. But Jesus is the best of all captains. And there are three great great things he has to help and comfort his soldiers that no other captain ever had in the same way.

In the first place, Jesus has GREAT KNOWLEDGE, *and for this reason he is the best Captain.*

No one can be a good captain to a company of soldiers unless he has a good deal of knowledge. He must know what sort of men the soldiers are; what sort of work they have to do; and what sort of help they need to enable them to do their work well. But Jesus has greater knowledge, about all these things, than any other captain ever had; and this is one thing that helps to make him the best Captain. He knows how to do every thing for them that they need to have done.

He knows how to feel for them when they are in trouble. This feeling for others we call *sympathy.*

THE VALUE OF SYMPATHY.

A minister of the gospel was sitting in his study one Saturday morning, busily engaged in writing his sermons for the next day. His little boy, about four years old, came toddling

into the room, and holding up his finger, which
had just been pinched by the door, with a look
of pain on his face, said : "Look, papa, how
I hurt my finger!" The father did not want
to be interrupted in his writing, so he merely
looked towards the child, and said, a little im-
patiently : "I can't help it, sonny." The little
fellow's eyes filled with tears ; and, as he turned
to go out, he said, in a low tone : "Yes, you
could : you might have said, 'Oh!'" That was
as good as a sermon. It would have been a
great comfort to that little fellow if his father
had stopped a moment, and said : "Oh! I'm
sorry ;" and then had tenderly kissed the hurt
finger. That father didn't know how to comfort
his child in his trouble. Mothers know how to
do this a great deal better than fathers do ; and
so, when Jesus wants to show us how well he
knows how to comfort his people in their
troubles, he says, "As one whom his *mother*
comforteth, so will I comfort you" (Isa. lxvi.
13).

But he knows how to *protect* them as well as
to comfort them.

THE BOY WHO GOT UP TO PRAY.

There was a little boy named Arthur. He was about six years old. He lived in England. His parents were both dead; and his uncle, who was a minister, took him home to live with him.

One winter's night, there was a fearful storm in that part of England. The wind was blowing terribly. Little Arthur's nurse took him to his room and undressed him. Then, as it was a cold night, he got into bed without saying his prayers, intending to say them in bed; he did so, but was not satisfied with it. He tossed about in his bed awhile, and listened to the howling of the wind, but could not go to sleep. He thought to himself that it was a mean sort of thing to say his prayers in bed, when God had been so good in taking care of him all the day. He could not feel comfortable about it; and so he resolved to get up and kneel down by the bedside, and say his prayers there, as he was in the habit of doing. Then he got up, and wrapped a shawl around him, and kneeled down in the usual place to offer up his prayers

to God.   As he was thus engaged, there came a
very violent gust of wind.   It blew down part
of a wall above the room in which Arthur slept.
With loud noise, a great stone came crashing
through the ceiling of his room, and fell on his
pillow, *just where his head would have been lying
if he had not got up to say his prayers!*   His
uncle rushed into the room, snatched him up in
his arms, and carried him over to his aunt's
room.   But they found he was not hurt in the
least.

" Oh, aunty!" he said, " I'm so glad that
God put it into my heart not to be afraid of the
dark or the cold ; for if I had not got up to say
my prayers that big stone would have fallen on
my head and killed me."

This shows us how Jesus, the Captain of our
salvation, uses the knowledge that he has for
the protection of his people.

And then Jesus knows how to *save* his people,
as well as to comfort and protect them.

THE BRANDS PLUCKED FROM THE FIRE.

Some years ago, two old people — a man and his wife — lived in an out-of-the-way part of the country in Virginia. The old man was an atheist, for he did not believe in the Bible, or in God. He had never been accustomed to go to church, and would not have a Bible in his house, or allow a minister to enter it. He was now confined to his bed with rheumatism; unable to help himself, while his wife still managed to creep about the house. Now think of their position. There they were, unable to go to church; with no Bible in their house, and without a minister or Christian friend to come near them: how was it possible for them to become Christians? You or I never could have made them such. But Jesus, the great Captain of our salvation, knew how to do it. The way in which he did it was very strange.

This was it. Two ministers of the gospel were travelling together on horseback through that part of the country. They intended to have turned off from the road along which they

were journeying, in order to visit a friend, whose
house was only a little way from the turn-
pike.

But, as they were earnestly engaged in conversation, they passed by the place without
knowing it, and rode on several miles beyond
it.   Then they stopped to talk about what they
had better do.   Just at that moment, they saw
a fire break out from the roof of a house by the
roadside.   They got off their horses and rushed
into the house.   It proved to be the very house
in which these old people lived.   The two
strangers arrived just in time to put out the
fire, which they did after a great deal of trouble,
and so saved the old people from being burnt
to death.

And when they found out that it was two
ministers of the gospel who had been the means
of saving them from that dreadful death, and
when they came to know about the singular
way in which those two good men came to be
there, at that very moment when the fire broke
out, it had a great effect upon their minds.   The
old man gave up his infidelity.   He saw that there

was a God, and that it was God who had sent
them help and saved their lives in that strange
way. He and his wife listened attentively
while the ministers read to them from the Bible,
and then talked to them about Jesus, and prayed
with them. And then the old wife got a Bible,
and read it regularly to her husband, and together they confessed their sins and prayed for
forgiveness. And God heard and answered their
prayers, and those wicked old people — in their
helplessness — became humble, earnest Christians, and died rejoicing in the hope which the
gospel gives. Jesus knew how to save those old
people, although their case seemed so hopeless.
He is the best of all captains, in the first place,
because he has great knowledge.

*He is the best Captain, in the second place, be-
cause he has* — GREAT POWER.

An earthly captain might be as strong as Samson was, and yet he could not give his own
strength to his soldiers. He could not make
them strong. But Jesus can do this. He
shares with his soldiers and people all the good
things that he has. And so we are encouraged

2

in the Bible by being told that God "has laid help on one who is mighty" (Ps. lxxxix. 19). And when we think how strong Jesus is, it is a great comfort to hear him say to each of us: "Fear not; I am with thee: I *will strengthen* thee; yea, I *will* HELP *thee*" (Isa. xli. 10). There are two occasions in which we especially need help. One is when we have duties to perform; the other when we have dangers to meet. In duty and in danger, Jesus can give us just the help we need.

LOVE MAKES THE DIFFERENCE.

James Wilson was a youth about seventeen years old. He had lately joined the church, or enlisted as a soldier in the army of Jesus. One day an old friend and former teacher met him, who had often spoken to him about becoming a Christian.

"Well, James," said he, "how are you getting on?"

"Very well, sir. Why it's just as different as can be."

"What is different?"

"Why, being a Christian. Every thing is so different from what I expected."

"Well, what did you expect?"

"Why, you see, when you used to talk to me about being a Christian, I would say to myself, 'No, I can't now; for I shall have to do so many hard things, that I am afraid to try it.'"

"What hard things?"

"Oh, I used to think, if I become a Christian, I shall have to go to church, and to meeting; shall have to pray, and to read the Bible, and be so careful about every thing. But I find it so different to what I thought!"

"Why, James, what do you mean?" asked his friend. "You *do* go to church, and to meeting; and you read your Bible, and pray, and try to do what you know is right in every thing, don't you?"

"Of course, I do," said James, looking up to his friend, with a sweet smile; "but then, you see, I *love* to do it now. And this makes all the difference. The fact is that I love Jesus. And, instead of it being a burden to do any thing for him, it is just the greatest pleasure I have to do what I know he wants me to do."

This is the way in which Jesus helps us in duty. And this is what he meant when he said : "My yoke is easy, and my burden is light." Nothing in the world is so pleasant as what we do for those we really love.

But Jesus is strong to help his people in *danger*, as well as in duty. And we need help especially at such times, because we have no strength to help ourselves.

TAKING SHELTER IN A DOORWAY.

If you are going along a crowded street, and see an open doorway, and just step into it, what a little thing that is! And yet here is a story to show how Jesus helped one of his people, when in danger, in just this way.

Some years ago, there was a poor woman who lived in the worst part of the great city of London, known as St. Giles. She lived by herself, in a miserable little room, for she had no relation in the world. She had never seen a Bible, and knew nothing about Jesus the great

Captain of our salvation, or about that glorious heaven that he is preparing for them that love him. She was tired of the wretched and miserable life that she was living. There was no prospect of any thing better for her; so she made up her mind to go to the river Thames, and drown herself, as many other poor, unhappy people have done. She put on her bonnet, and started for the river. As she went slowly along, at one place there was a crowd of people on the narrow pavement. The crowd was coming towards her. There was a door open at her right hand. To get out of the way of the crowd, she stepped into the open door, without thinking what she was doing. Now Jesus had so ordered it, that, in the room to which that open door led, there should then be a Bible-reader engaged in his blessed work. He had gathered a few of the people of that wretched neighborhood around him, and was reading to them from the New Testament. He happened to be reading then the eleventh chapter of St. Matthew; and, just as this poor woman stepped into that open door, he read the twenty-eighth verse of that chapter. This is it: "*Come unto me, all ye that labor, and are heavy laden, and I will give you rest.*" Maria — this was the poor woman's name — started when she heard that verse read. It seemed to her that the words it contained were the sweetest words she had ever heard. She said to herself: "Who can it be that speaks such beautiful words? '*Weary and heavy-laden,*' why that's just what I *am*. '*Rest*'? why that's just what I *want*. That's better than drowning. I must find out about this."

Then she made up her mind not to go to the river. She stepped quietly into the room, and sat down to hear what more the Bible-reader had to say. When the meeting was over she had a long talk with him. He gave her a Testament, and asked her to come to his meeting every day. She came; she listened; she read; she prayed. Jesus heard her prayers. She found rest, and peace, and joy in him. And now, for years past, she has been engaged herself as a Bible-reader in that same neighborhood, and has done a wonderful deal of good.

A MAN OVERBOARD.

A lady who was on board the vessel where the event took place, of which I am now to speak, gives this account of it.

Our ship was coming from the Sandwich Islands, round by China and the Cape of Good Hope to New York. One day we were going along with a good fresh breeze when, all at once, while sitting on deck, I heard a loud cry of — " Man overboard ! " " Man overboard ! " One of the crew had fallen into the water. The passengers rushed up from the cabin, and the sailors ran about on deck. For a while, there was a great noise and confusion. But in a few moments it was all over; and the captain walked quietly back to the quarter-deck, and said to one of the passengers : " It was one of the sailors, who was painting the ship's side. He slipped into the water ; but he had a rope fast to him, so we pulled him out, and he got no harm but a ducking."

It is customary with sailors, when working on the side of the vessel, as that man was doing, to have a rope fastened round the waist. The other end of the rope is made fast on deck, so that if a man falls into the water, he is really in no danger of being lost. For he has but to call out to his friends on deck, and they can haul him up by the rope.

And this illustrates the way in which Jesus uses his great power for the safety of his people. They are exposed to the danger of falling into the snares and temptations of the world, and into sin. These are about us all the time, just as the waters of the sea are round about a vessel. But the power of Jesus, or his love and grace, are like the rope fastened to the sailor, and which kept him from being lost. We read of good men in the Bible who fell into sin. It was so with Abraham, and Moses, and David, and Peter. When they sinned, it was like the sailor falling overboard. But Jesus had the rope of his grace and power round them. He did not let them perish, but drew them out of the water, and brought them safely on board the vessel again.

Somebody has beautifully set forth the great

power of Jesus to help his people, by showing
some of the many ways in which he can use the
two little words, *I Am*, in reference to himself. We can think of Jesus as speaking to
each of his people in this way: —

> "I am thy God; there's none beside:
> I am thy rock, thy shield, thy guide:
> I am thy portion; trust in me;
> My promise I will keep with thee:
> I am thy strength, sufficient, sure:
> I am thy refuge; rest secure:
> I am thy fortress, there abide,
> Safe when the ills of life betide:
> I am thy sun, thy path to light:
> I am the door; I lead aright:
> I am the Shepherd; mine I know;
> They follow where my footsteps go:
> I am the way; come unto me:
> I am the truth, that maketh free:
> I am the life, and life I give,
> That dying men may look and live:
> I am thy crown; fear not, endure:
> I am alive for evermore:
> I am the first and last as well,
> And have the keys of death and hell!"

Jesus is indeed the best Captain because he
has great power.

And then there is another reason why Jesus

*may well be called the best Captain, and this is be-
cause he has* — GREAT SUCCESS.

A victory is a great thing for a captain. And
when he gains a number of victories, one after
another, it encourages his soldiers, and they feel
ready to do any thing for such a captain. But
no captain ever had so many victories as Jesus,
our great Captain, has had. He never lost a
battle. He always succeeds in every thing he
undertakes to do. And he is not only successful in what he does himself, but he makes his
soldiers or people successful too. We have
plenty of illustrations of this in the Bible. We
have one of these in Gideon, of which we read
in the book of Judges. He was a soldier of
Jesus, and his success was wonderful. He had
a little band of only three hundred men. That
was a mere handful. Yet he led them forth to
fight an army of Midianites that numbered one
hundred and thirty-five thousand men! This
army was four hundred and fifty times as large
as Gideon's little band. And yet Gideon was
successful in defeating that vast army.

And then there was that great Philistine

giant, Goliath of Gath. He defied the army of Israel. All the bravest soldiers in that army were afraid of him. Not one of them dared to go and fight him. But David, the shepherd boy of Bethlehem, went against him. The giant was covered all over with armor. He had a huge sword at his side, and a great spear in his hand, the staff of which was like a weaver's beam. David had never been in battle before. He had no shield, no armor, and no sword. He had nothing in his hand but a sling, and, in a bag that hung by his side, a few pebble stones from the brook. How very unlikely it seemed that he would be able to conquer that great giant under such circumstances! But he went out against him, trusting in Jesus, the Captain of our salvation; and He made him successful. With one stone, thrown from his sling, he brought the proud giant to the ground; and then, with the giant's own sword, he smote him, and cut off his head. It was Jesus who gave David his famous victory over the giant.

Now let me give one or two examples from our own times, of the way in which Jesus gives

success to those who are working for him, when
it seems impossible for them to succeed.

PASTORAL PERSEVERANCE.

A faithful minister of the gospel had an
elderly man belonging to his parish, who took
no interest in religion, and who seldom went
to church.   The minister had tried faithfully
to get him to come to church, and to have him
become a Christian; but all in vain.   At last
the man was taken sick, and confined to his
bed.   When he heard of this, the minister
called on him.   On entering the cottage, he
asked to see him.   The old man heard him up
in his room, and recognizing his voice called
out rudely: "I don't want you here, you can
go away."

The next day the minister called again, and
going to the foot of the stairs, he said: "Well,
my good friend, may I come up and see you
to-day?"

The angry reply was: "No; I don't want
you here."

Now this case seemed hopeless.   Most men

would have given it up in despair, feeling that it was not worth while to try any more. But this good man thought differently. He concluded to continue his visits. Every day for twenty-one successive days he called regularly. In the same kind manner he asked how the sick man was, and if he would see him to-day, and every day he received the same rude answer: "No; I don't want to see you."

But when he called the twenty-second time, the sick man's manner changed. His rough voice was softened, and he said: "Come up, if you please, sir: I want to see you."

Then he visited him every day. He read the Bible to him. He talked to him about Jesus, and prayed with him. It pleased God to make the old man well again. But he was a very different man, after his sickness, from what he was before. He went regularly to church, and became an earnest Christian.

It seemed impossible that this minister should have succeeded in this case. But it was Jesus, the great Captain of our salvation, who made him successful.

Suppose that we should see a drunken man go staggering into church : should we expect him to get any good from going there in that state? No; of course not. And yet, let me tell you of just such a case, which occurred not long ago, and in which Jesus, the Captain of our salvation, made the service of that day the means of saving the man's soul. This is the story : —

One Sunday, a poor drunken man walked into a large and well-filled church, during the service. He came in while they were singing the first hymn, and took a seat near the pulpit. His shabby appearance, and unsteady walk, drew the attention of the congregation towards him. As soon as the minister began to preach, the stranger fell asleep. Then he began to snore, and pretty soon he was snoring so loud that the minister could not be heard distinctly. One of the officers of the church rose to lead the man out of the building. But the minister stopped a moment, and said : —

"Let him alone, if you please. He does not disturb me. If he disturbs you, try and bear with him. I hope he may hear something before he leaves that may do him good. He didn't know what he was doing when he came in here. I believe the Lord has sent him. Let him stay."

The man continued to sleep on, but more quietly. When the next hymn was given out, and the organ began to play, the sound woke him. He started to his feet, and looked round in astonishment. It was that grand old hymn, "Rock of Ages," that they were singing. It seemed to have a strange effect upon him. He sat down, and covered his face with his hands. Those who were near could see the tears flowing through his fingers. The secret of it was, that he had had a pious mother. She had taught him that hymn when a child. He had not heard it for years. It brought up the memory of his mother now in heaven, and this was the cause of his deep feeling.

The next Sunday he was there again; but he was sober then. He became a regular attendant and an earnest listener there. Before long he joined the church, and became an humble, earnest Christian.

And now see how wonderfully Jesus, the Captain of our salvation, ordered things so as to secure the salvation of this man's soul. He gave him a pious mother to pray for him. She died, and went to heaven; without seeing her prayers answered. But they were not forgotten. I would rather have the prayers of a pious mother to follow me, than have all the money that any one could leave me. Jesus remembered those prayers. He followed that wicked son in his drunken ways. He drew him into church, that day, by the sound of the organ. The sound of the organ woke him from his sleep. Then that hymn reminded him of his mother, softened his heart, and led him to repentance; and so his mother's prayers were answered, and his soul was saved. What a successful Captain Jesus is!

And so we see there are three good reasons why he may be called the best Captain. The first is, because he has great knowledge; the second, because he has great power; and the third, because he has great success.

When we enter the church of Christ by baptism, we are enlisted under his banner, and are pledged to "fight manfully against sin, the world, and the devil, and to continue Christ's faithful soldiers and servants unto our life's end." Let us always remember that Jesus is our Captain, and let us pray for all the grace we need, that we may show ourselves to be "good soldiers of Jesus Christ."

II.

THE BEST OF ALL BLESSINGS.

"The best of Blessings." — PAGE 56.

II.

THE BEST OF ALL BLESSINGS.

" All the things thou canst desire are not to be compared unto her." — PROVERBS iii. 15.

SOLOMON is speaking of religion here. He calls her wisdom. Then he says " She is more precious than rubies." And he is going on to speak about religion still, when he says : " All the things thou canst desire are not to be compared unto her." This is a wonderful saying. It is very much like what Jesus said one day while on earth, when he asked this solemn question : " What shall it profit a man if he gain the whole world and lose his own soul ? or what shall a man give in exchange for his soul ? " This is very much like our text. In that passage, Jesus does in substance say that all things one can desire are not to be compared unto the soul : just as, in our text, Solomon says : " All things thou canst desire are not to be compared unto her:" that is, unto wisdom; or unto religion; or unto the grace of God. What shall a man give in exchange for his soul? or what shall a man give in exchange for the grace of God?

This is the greatest question we can ever have to answer. It refers to the most important thing that we shall have to do with in all our lives. And it is a question just as important for one person as for another. It is as important for you as for me. It is as important for the rich man as for the poor man; as important for the king upon his throne as for the beggar in his garret. When Jesus asked: "What shall a man give in exchange for his soul?" it seems as if he had held up a huge pair of scales before us. They reach up to the heavens. In one side of the scales, he puts a soul,— an immortal soul, like yours or mine. In the other side, he puts the whole world. He is weighing them before our eyes, to let us see which is the heaviest, or which is worth the most. But there, see, the side which has the soul in it sinks down in a moment, while the side which

has the world in it flies up and strikes the
beam.   It seems as if there were but a feather
on one side of the scales; while, on the other
side, was a great mass of solid gold.

And Solomon seems to be doing the same
thing in our text.   It is as if he had such a pair
of scales before him.   He puts religion on one
side, and "all things that can be desired" on the
other side.   And religion turns the scale in this
case, just as the soul did in the former case.
"All the things thou canst desire are not to be
compared unto her."   The meaning of this is,
that religion is worth more than every thing
else.   There is nothing to be compared to religion.   "All the things that thou canst desire!"
only think what this means.   Now suppose that
you and I just try our hand at desiring, or wish-
ing, and see what sort of a pile we can make.
Well, we can desire, or wish for, all the money
in the banks of Philadelphia, New York and
Boston, of London and Paris; and all the gold
and silver in the world.   We can desire, or
wish for, all the rubies and the diamonds, all
the gems and jewels, all the houses and lands,

all the books and paintings, all the thrones
and sceptres, all the beauty of the prettiest persons and all the wisdom of the wisest persons,
in the world. And suppose we not only wished
for these things, but had them. Suppose that
we were stronger than Samson, and wiser than
Solomon, and richer than Crœsus, and more
beautiful than an angel; suppose that all the
crowns in the world could be melted down into
one, and that one put upon our head, and we
were made the owner and ruler of the globe, —
yet, without religion, all this would be of no
worth to us. We might set these things, even
" all that we can desire," on the one hand, and
religion on the other, and Solomon says : " *They*
are not to be compared unto *her.*"

Perhaps some of you are hardly willing to believe this. But it is just as true as it is that
two and two make four. I wish to give you
three good reasons to prove that this is so.

" All the things that thou canst desire are not
to be compared unto her," or unto the grace of
God. This is true,

In the first place, because WE CANNOT GET ALL

THAT WE DESIRE, BUT WE CAN GET THE GRACE
OF GOD.

People desire a great many things in this
world which they can never get.

We begin very soon to desire, or wish for
things that cannot be gotten; and then we feel
unhappy, because we cannot get them. Here,
for instance, is a nurse, with a baby in her arms.
She is walking on the porch of the house, on
the evening of a calm summer's day. The sun
has set in the west; and yonder, in the east,
the full moon, bright and clear, is sailing up the
sky. The baby sees the beautiful moon. It
wants to have it. It stretches out its little
hands in the earnest desire to get it. But it is
desiring what cannot be had, and presently it
bursts into a bitter cry, the cry of disappointment, on finding that it cannot get one of the
things it has desired. Perhaps that is the baby's
first lesson in the school of life. It is just beginning to learn that there are many things that we
can desire in this world, but which cannot be
had.

Some time since, a gentleman was going along

a road in the country. On the grassy bank by the roadside, sat a little boy, eight or nine years old, crying as if his heart would break. The gentleman supposed, of course, that the little fellow was in some great trouble. He thought to himself, as he was coming up to him, " Poor child ! perhaps he has lost his way ; or perhaps he has been without food all day, and now is crying for hunger ; or perhaps some hard-hearted person has been beating and ill treating him, and he may be crying for pain." At any rate, the gentleman felt sorry for the child, and resolved to stop and find out the cause of his grief, and see if he could do any thing to comfort him. So he went up to him, and, speaking kindly, said : " What is the matter with you, my little man ? "

The boy looked up into his face, while the tears streamed down his cheeks, and with a voice choked with sobs exclaimed : " O dear ! what shall I do ? I *can't make my kite go up.*" The gentleman spoke a few kind words to the little fellow, and then went on his way. But, as he did this, he thought to himself : How many people there are in the world just like this little boy! They have some kite or other which they are trying to fly. There is something they desire to do, or to get. But they do not succeed. They cannot make their kite go up. It is one of " the things that they desire," to have it go up; but it cannot be done, and this gives them trouble.

One day, during harvest, two farmer boys were resting at dinner-time, under a fine shady tree. One of them was named Bob; the other was named Tom. They were stretched out on the grass, talking pleasantly together. "I say, Bob," said Tom, who was lying on his back, gazing listlessly up to the sky, "I'll tell you what I wish; I wish I had a farm as big as all that blue sky yonder. I'd have half of it in forest or woodlands, and the other half of it in nice meadow lands. Wouldn't I be somebody then, old chap?" and he fairly chuckled and clapped his hands for joy at the mere thought of being so well off. This was the thing that Tom desired.

"Good for you, Tom," said Bob; "but I tell

you what I wish. I wish I had as many cattle as there are leaves in yonder woods. I'd be better off than you, Mr. Tom, with your big sky-blue farm. I'd be the richest man in this county, by a long piece."

" I'm not quite so sure about that, Bob," said Tom. " But suppose now you had all those cattle, what would you do with them ? "

" Why I'd put them to pasture in your big meadows, to be sure."

" But suppose I wouldn't let you. What then ? "

" Why then I'd make you: that's all."

" You couldn't do it."

" That is a lie." Then came a blow, and the boys fell to fighting. There was nobody at hand to separate them, so they fought till they were tired. Then they stopped to take breath. While they were resting, Tom began to think of the folly of their conduct. " Bob," said he, " what are we quarrelling about ? "

" Why about pasturing your cattle in my meadows."

" But I haven't got any cattle, and you

haven't any meadows. What fools we are! Give me your hand, Bob." So they made up, and were good friends again. Now you see the things which these boys desired were cattle and farms; but, with all their desire, they could not get them.

Do you remember the fable about the proud frog? The fable says that this frog, as he sat by the edge of the pond, looked with great admiration on a huge ox that was feeding in the field. He thought, how grand it must be to be as big as that! Then he began to wish that he was as big as the ox. He tried to hold his breath, and puff himself up to the same size. After trying for a while, he said to a companion at his side, "Am I not almost as big as that ox?" "Pooh! nonsense," said his friend. The frog tried again and again, and asked, each time, if he was not then up to the mark. But still the answer would be: "No; not at all. Nothing like it." At last he made one tremendous effort, and burst his skin in making it, and died. You see, the thing which the frog desired was what he could not get. If religion

or the grace of God is the thing we desire, it is something within our reach. God
says, in reference to it, "Ask, and ye shall receive ; seek, and ye shall find." If we desire
this, we can get it ; but if we desire other
things we may not be able to get them.
And this shows us that the saying of Solomon in our text is true. We cannot get all
that we desire, but we can get the grace of God.

But the second reason that proves the truth of
what Solomon here says is, that, IF WE COULD
GET ALL THE THINGS THAT WE DESIRE, THEY
WOULD NOT MAKE US HAPPY, BUT THE GRACE
OF GOD WILL.

We often see people desiring to get certain
things. They set their hearts on getting them,
and when they do get them they are no happier than they were before. A peasant boy
sees a nest on the top of a high tree. He desires to get the nest. He thinks about it by
day, and dreams about it by night. At length
he resolves to climb the tree and secure the
nest. At the risk of breaking his neck, he goes
up the tree ; he seizes the nest, and finds it

empty. There is nothing in it to reward him for his toil and danger.

There is a prince who, like Richard the Third of England, wants to be made king. He desires to gain a crown. He is ready to do any thing, no matter how wicked, in order to gain his end. If anybody stands in his way, he will not hesitate a moment to murder him. He goes steadily onward till he gains the crown. He gets what he desired, and then finds himself the most unhappy man in the land. We often hear people talk about being " as happy as a king." This is a great mistake. Kings are not, by any means, the happiest people in the world. One of the greatest writers who ever lived, and one who knew a great deal about kings, when speaking of them, said : —

"*Uneasy* lies the head that wears a crown."

And we know that this is generally the case. When we come to read the lives of kings, we find that, for the most part, they are not happy. There is David, the king of Israel. He was one of the best kings that ever lived. He was a truly pious man ; and yet we hear him exclaiming: " O that I had wings like a dove, for then would I flee away and be at rest!" This shows that *his* head was uneasy, although it wore a crown. Dionysius was the king of Sicily. He was a rich and powerful king; but, when he was talking with a friend one day about his position, he said he felt just like a person who was moving about with a sharp, glittering sword hanging by a single hair over his head. Now that, I should think, was a very uneasy position to be in. Who would want to wear the brightest crown on earth, if he had to feel as Dionysius felt all the time?

When Nicholas, the late Emperor of Russia, travelled in Italy, he was in constant fear of being killed. When he stopped at any place at night, during his journey, he was afraid to go to bed till he had taken a hammer and pounded on the walls all round the room, to find out if they were solid. He was afraid there might be some closet, or secret place, where some murderer might be hid away, waiting for a chance to come out and kill him while he was sleeping. Who would care to wear a crown if, in consequence of it, he had to live in such a state of uneasiness as this ?

The lives of kings afford us the most striking illustrations of this part of our subject, because, on account of their position, they are able to get more of the things that people desire in this world than others can.

There is Solomon, for instance. He was, perhaps, the richest king that ever lived; and he got for himself " all the things that can be desired " to give people pleasure in this world. He built magnificent palaces ; he made beautiful gardens, in which were all sorts of fruits, and flowers, and fountains ; he had gold and silver, and gems, and jewels, and men singers, and women singers. All things that his eye, or his ear, or his heart desired, he got for himself. He tried them all; and, when he got through, what had he to say of them ? These were his words: " Vanity of vanities, ALL *is vanity !* "

Alexander desired to conquer the world. He did conquer it. He got what he desired. But was he satisfied ? Ah, no! or else he would not have cried for more worlds to conquer. He would not have set fire to a great city, and have died when drunk, at a feast.

Julius Cæsar desired to be a great conqueror. He gained his desire. He conquered eight hundred cities. He was the means of killing more than a million of his enemies, and then he was murdered in the senate chamber, where he was hoping to enjoy the honors he had won.

There was once a celebrated king of ancient Spain. His reign had been very long, and very splendid. Before he died, he said to a particular friend one day: "I have kept a record of all the happy days I have spent, during my reign of sixty years, and in looking over that record to see how many such days I have had, I find there only" — how many do you think? — "*only one!*"

But others, besides kings and emperors, get "the things they have desired," and yet find that these cannot make them happy. If you ever go to England, and should land at Liverpool, you will find, at the Exchange in that town, a splendid bronze monument to Lord Nelson. And in many of the public places throughout the kingdom, you will find some monument or memorial of the same great man. Lord Nelson was, in early life, a poor sickly boy. He entered the British Navy as a boy without friends, and without much prospect of ever becoming a great man. But he desired very much to distinguish himself as one of the naval heroes of England. He did so. He toiled hard and long for fame, honor, and wealth. He gained them all. That poor pale-faced boy rose to the highest place in the English Navy. He became a knight of various orders, an admiral, a viscount, a lord, a duke. He was the hero of a hundred fights. Whole nations feared him. In his native land no man was ever more honored than he. He was literally covered with the glory of this world. "All the things that he had desired" he gained. But did they make him happy? Judge for yourself from what he said. One day, while writing to a friend he used these words: "I am now perfectly the great man.

No one stands near me in honor. *Yet, from my heart, I wish myself the little man again !*"

An Arab once lost his way in the wilderness, and was in danger of perishing from hunger. He had been a jeweller by profession, and there was nothing he had desired more than the possession of pearls, and precious things. But now, he was in great distress for food. At last he came to one of the cisterns, out of which the camels were accustomed to drink. Lying by the cistern, he saw a leathern bag. Supposing it contained dates or nuts, he sprang forward with great eagerness to seize it, exclaiming, as he did so: "God be thanked! here are some dates or nuts, so that I may eat and be refreshed!" He opened the bag, but only to turn away in disappointment. It was full of — *only* pearls! They were the very things he had been in the habit of desiring more than any thing else. But they were not what he wanted then. He was on the point of starving. What good would these pearls do him? He would gladly have exchanged them all for a handful of food. Here were the things he had desired in great abundance, but they could not make him happy.

I will only mention one other case to show that persons may succeed in getting the things they have desired, and yet be very far from being happy. Everybody, who lives in Philadelphia, has heard something about Stephen Girard. He was the richest man in that city when he was living. He founded and owned the bank in Third Street, known as the Girard Bank. He left all the money required to build, and support, the Girard College for orphans, on the Ridge Road. This is, I suppose, the most costly and beautiful building in this country, next to the capitol at Washington. In his early days, Stephen Girard was very poor. But the thing he desired was to be rich. He felt, I suppose, as many people do, that if he could only get plenty of money he would be satisfied and happy. In the course of time, he became rich. When he died, it was reckoned that he was worth about fifteen millions of dollars. This was more money than he knew what to do with. In writing to a friend one day, he said:

"As for myself, I live like a galley-slave. I have no enjoyment of my riches, and am worn out with the care of them. To be constantly engaged in work is my highest pleasure. When I rise in the morning, my only desire is to work so hard all day, that at night I may sleep soundly." There you see the rich man, who had gained "all the things he could desire" in the way of money, and yet was not made happy by it.

But, if we seek the grace of God, it will certainly make us happy. Whether we are rich or poor; whether we are sick or well, — we shall have enough to make us happy, if we only have the grace of God in our hearts. And this is the second reason why "all the things that we can desire are not to be compared" unto the grace of God: *they* cannot make us happy if we get them, — but *this* can.

But there is a third reason why the words of Solomon in the text are true. "All the things thou canst desire are not to be compared unto" the grace of God, *because if we could get them, and if they could make us happy,* WE CANNOT

KEEP THEM; BUT WE CAN KEEP THE GRACE OF
GOD.

You know how the sky, under which we live,
is changing all the time : you can hardly ever
look at it twice when it presents exactly the
same appearance. The world in which we live
is turning round and round, or upsidedown
continually ; and it is just so with the things of
the world. Like the clouds in the sky, they
are changing, and passing away all the time.

There was a celebrated king of Egypt once,
whose name was Sesostris. He was a great
warrior and conqueror. In one of the wars in
which he was engaged, he conquered and took
captive four kings. On his return, when entering the capital of his kingdom, he had these four
kings harnessed to his chariot, that they might
drag it for him, in place of the horses by which
it was usually drawn. As they were going
along, he noticed that one of the kings was
watching very closely the wheel of one of
the chariots. His eye was fixed very steadily
upon it, and he seemed to be engaged in the
deepest thought. Sesostris ordered the chariot

to stop, and then asked this captive what was the meaning of his looking so earnestly at that wheel ? He replied : " When I look upon that wheel, and see what changes are taking place in it continually ; how that part which is the lowest at one time is the highest at another, and that which is the highest now is presently the lowest, — it puts me in mind of our fortune in this life, and the changes which are taking place continually. Yesterday I was at the top of the wheel, and now I am at the bottom of it." Sesostris was so struck with this thought that he unfastened the captive kings from his chariot, and gave them their liberty.

There was once a great warrior whose name was Amor. He had been very successful in his wars, and had conquered all Persia and Tartary. But at last he was defeated in battle, and taken prisoner. At the close of the day he was very hungry. While sitting on the ground, waiting for a soldier to prepare him something to eat, in the rough way in which prisoners are often treated, there came a hungry dog along. He thrust his head into the pan which con-

tained the meat intended for the captive general.
The mouth of this vessel was so small that,
when the dog had thrust his head into it, he
could not easily get it out again. Feeling
alarmed at the predicament in which he found
himself, he concluded he had better retreat;
so he took to his heels, and off he ran, as hard
as he could go, carrying pan, and meat, and all,
away with him. When Amor, the captive general, saw this he burst into a fit of laughter.
Some one, who had not witnessed the dog's pro-
ceedings, asked him, what led one in his situation to be so merry! His reply was: "Look
at yonder dog. It was only this morning that
the steward of my household came to me, and
complained that three hundred camels were
not sufficient to carry all my kitchen furni-
ture; but now, you see, it can all be carried by
that dog, who has run off at once, both with my
dinner, and the vessel in which it was to be
cooked."

Now suppose that this general had gained all
the victories, and made all the conquests, he had
ever desired to gain or to make; and suppose he

had been perfectly happy in his conquests, yet if he could not keep them, but had to lose them so soon, what was the use of them?

You know how very slender the silk-like thread is, with which the spider weaves its web. It is so fine that you can hardly see it. And yet, it has been well said, that even this is stronger than the tie by which we hold the riches and possessions of this world. Suppose you have a fine farm. As you are walking over it, you see a large flock of birds that have lighted on the trees, or are picking up food in the field. You call them *your* birds, because they are on your farm. But can you tell how long you will have them? No. You have no power to hold them. At any moment, they may rise on the wing, and disappear, you know not where. And it is just so with the wealth, and honors, and other things of this world which people have. The Bible tells us that " riches *take to themselves wings and fly away.*" The money, you call your own, is not absolutely yours, because it happens, just now, to be in your hand, or pocket, or drawer, or bank, any more than those birds are

absolutely yours, because they happen, at this
moment, to be lighting on your trees, or feeding
in your meadow.

You are all familiar with the name of Saladin, the celebrated sultan and leader of the
Saracens. He lived in the twelfth century, at
the time of the Crusaders. The Turks and
Saracens — the infidels as they were called —
had possession of the Holy Land with the city
of Jerusalem. The Christian nations of Europe
thought it was a shame, that the city of Jerusalem, and the tomb in which our blessed
Saviour was buried, should be in the hands of
men who were the enemies of his religion. So
they raised great armies, and sent them to
Palestine, to fight for the possession of that
land again. This led to long and bloody wars.
In these wars, Saladin was one of the best and
bravest warriors among the Saracens. He had
scarcely an equal on either side of the contending
armies, except in Richard, the lion-hearted King
of England. Saladin was a great prince, a great
warrior, and a great man. He had acquired
great wealth. He had gained great honor and dis-

tinction. He had every thing that a brave and successful soldier could have to make him happy. Perhaps he was happy in a certain way. But, after a while, the time drew near when he was to die. His battles had all been fought. His splendid victories had all been gained. He was lying on his couch sick, and pale, and panting for breath. The princes and peers, the warriors and nobles, of his kingdom were gathered round him. He ordered the shroud to be brought in which his lifeless body would soon be wrapped up. The dying Saladin told one of his officers to take that shroud, and fasten it to the end of his victorious banner-staff, and then to put it into the hands of one of his heralds, and send him through the streets of the city, proclaiming as he went: " *This is all that is left, of all his greatness, to the mighty Saladin !* " He had gained the things that he desired, and he had found enjoyment in them, *but he could not keep them.* This is our last reason why "all things that thou canst desire are not to be compared unto" the grace of God.

Thus we have given three reasons to show the truth of what Solomon says in our text. It is true in the first place, because we cannot get all the things that we desire, but we can get the the grace of God. It is true in the second place, because if we could get all the things we can desire they would not make us happy, but the grace of God will. And it is true in the third place, because if we could get all the things we can desire, and if they could make us happy, we cannot keep them; but we can keep the grace of God.

And if we believe what Solomon here tells us, that the grace of God, or the religion of Jesus, is the most valuable thing in the world, then how earnestly we should seek it! We may desire and seek after many things in this world, but never get them. But if we desire to love and serve Jesus, and seek his grace to help us, we shall certainly get what we seek! This is especially true, if we begin to seek him while we are young. There is a sweet promise to help us in doing this. Jesus says: "I love them that love me, and *those who seek me early shall find me.*" And if we find him, we shall be happy for ever. Let us pray earnestly to Jesus to change our hearts, and make us his children, and servants. Then we shall have that wisdom, or that grace of God, which is "more precious than rubies," and than "all the things that can be desired."

III.

HOW THE BIRDS PRAISE GOD.

"How the Birds praise God." — Page 86.

III.

HOW THE BIRDS PRAISE GOD.

" Behold the fowls of the air." — MATTHEW vii. 26.

HERE Jesus makes the birds our teachers.

We love to see the birds, and hear them. It is very interesting, and instructive, to study their history and habits. We can learn many useful lessons from them. Jesus sends us to the birds to learn how to trust God. He says they have no harvests to gather, and no barns full of food to depend upon, and yet they do not fret, or worry. They sing away merrily all the time, and trust God to provide for them the food they will require. This is the one particular lesson which Jesus speaks of the birds as teaching in our text. But there are more lessons than this, that the birds teach us. We wish to learn some of these lessons. In the one hundred and forty-eighth Psalm, David calls on the birds, or the flying fowl, as he calls them, to praise God. And

5

this is what we are now to speak about. Our
subject is, *how the birds praise God.*

I wish to speak of *four* ways in which they
do this.

In the first place, the birds praise God by —
THE WAY THEY LIVE.

Some birds are not able to fly much. They
spend their lives in walking about the earth.
This is the case with our chickens and barn-
yard fowls. And it is so with the ostrich in
the desert. His wings are of little use to him,
when he is pursued by his enemies ; but look
at his legs, and see how well fitted they are for
running ! He can go faster than a horse, and
almost as fast as the wind.

Some birds live by wading in the water, and
it is interesting to see how wonderfully God has
fitted them for just that kind of life. They are
furnished with very long legs, by which they
can go through the shallow water, near the
banks of rivers and lakes ; and their necks are
long and slender, too, so that they can easily
reach down to the bottom of the water, and
search for the food which they find there.

The flamingo is an example of this class of birds.

Then there are other kinds of birds that live a great deal on the water. They swim over its surface, or dive into its depths and find their principal food there. And if you take a duck or a goose as a specimen of birds of this kind, and compare it with one of those wading birds that we were just speaking of, you will see what a wonderful difference there is between them. The long, flat body of the duck, with its short legs and web feet, are just as well adapted for swimming as the long legs of the heron or crane are for wading.

But we generally think of the birds as made for flying. We speak of them as "the birds of the air." The air is their natural home: there they spend the greater part of their lives, and find their greatest enjoyment. And nothing shows the wisdom of God more than the way in which he has fitted the birds to live in the air, and feel at home there. Every bird is a sort of flying machine. Men have been trying for a long time to make a machine of this sort, but they never have succeeded. They have made balloons, indeed, that will rise up into the air, and sail through it; but they are unable to steer them, or guide them, and so they are of little use. But God has filled the air with live flying machines in the form of birds, from the tiny humming-bird up to the great, lordly eagle, or the condor, that finds its home on the Andes. And these machines are wonderfully perfect in every part.

If we were trying to make a machine that would fly, we should want to have it as *light* as possible, and yet as strong as we could make it. And God has been very careful in securing these two things, in making his flying machines, the birds. The body of a bird is made very light. The bones are all made hollow. They are as light, and yet as strong, as it is possible to make them. And then to make them lighter still, God has arranged it so that the air passes into all the bones in a bird's body. This is the case down even to the small bones of the toes, to the quills of the feathers, and the tips of the wings. And then, besides the air in the bones

of a bird, there are sacks or cells for containing
air, in different parts of the body. These are
all connected with the lungs by which the bird
breathes. Through these it controls them, and
can fill them, and empty them just as it pleases.
And when these bones and bags are all filled
with air, the body of a bird is ready to rise and
sail away like a balloon full of gas. It floats
in the air almost as easily as a piece of cork
floats on the water. We sometimes see sea-
gulls, and other birds of considerable size, sailing about, with their outspread wings, and
seeming to be as much at their ease as a baby
is when rocked in its cradle. The condor, of
the Andes, is one of the largest birds we know
of, and yet its body is made so light by the air
it carries in it, that it can sail around for hours
without ever once flapping its wings. The frigate
bird is another very large bird. Sometimes its
wings, when spread out, measure fifteen feet
from one end to the other. And yet these birds
are often seen by our sailors, out at sea, a thousand miles from land. They seldom go ashore
for any thing but to lay their eggs. They

scarcely ever rest on the water. The air is their home. They live, and move, and have their being there. They eat, and drink, and work, and play, and rest, and sleep while sailing about on their broad, outspread wings. How nicely balanced their bodies must be to enable them to do this !

Some birds fly very fast, and very far; and it would be impossible for them to do this unless their bodies were made both very light, and very strong. Thirty miles an hour is reckoned very slow for a bird. The swallow is said to fly at the rate of ninety miles an hour, and the hawk a hundred and fifty miles an hour. This is very fast flying.

And these birds sometimes fly very far at a time. Some birds migrate, or travel from one country to another every year. When winter comes, they go to a warmer country; and when spring returns they come back again. In the south of Europe certain birds always go over to Africa in the fall. They spend the winter there, and return in the spring. When the time comes for one of these journeys, they all meet together in some place, and have a sort of bird convention. A great chattering is kept up, as though they were talking and making speeches to each other. When they get through with this, they appoint a leader, and arrange themselves in order, and start. They have to travel for hundreds of miles, all the way across the Mediterranean Sea. They have no map or compass, no landmark or finger-board, by which to steer their way. Yet they never make a mistake. There is no place for them to stop at on their journey. They can neither rest nor sleep, nor eat nor drink, till they get through; and yet they are able to do this twice a year without any trouble. How wonderful this is! When we think of the birds having their home, some on the land, some on the water, and some in the air; when we think how light their bodies are, and yet how strong; how easily they move about in the air, and how much comfort and enjoyment they seem to have in it, — then, when we "behold the fowls of the air," we may well say that they praise God, in the first place, by *the way they live.*

In the second place, the birds praise God by the WAY THEY DRESS.

The dress of birds is made up of their feathers. And there are *three* things about this dress which show God's wisdom and goodness, and by which it may well be said that they praise him.

It is a *warm* dress. And the birds need to have just such a dress. You know when you are riding in an open wagon, how cold you get by going rapidly through the air. But when the birds are flying, they go through the air much faster than we can ever go by riding. And this would soon make them feel very cold, if God had not taken great pains to protect them from the cold. But he has furnished them with clothing made of nice soft down and feathers. These are very light, and at the same time very warm. And so, though they have to go very rapidly through the cold air, the dress which God has provided for them keeps them warm and comfortable. It is a warm dress which the birds wear.

At the same time it is a *waterproof* dress.

All the birds do not need this kind of a dress, and all do not have it. Some, like our domestic fowls, have no occasion to go into the water; and their dress is not waterproof. If you see a chicken that is exposed to a heavy shower of rain, or that has fallen into a pond, you know how bedraggled its feathers become. They soak up the water like a rag, and become very heavy. But it is different with the birds that are accustomed to the water. Look at the ducks and geese, and the beautiful swans. They dive in the water, or sail about over it all day, and never get the least wet. And how is this done? Why God has given them an oily substance which they spread over their feathers, and which makes them entirely waterproof. And so many birds, that live on the water, where it is as cold as ice, are able to swim about all day, and yet be as dry and comfortable as can be, because of the warm waterproof clothing that God has prepared for them.

And then when you think how *beautiful* the dress of the birds is, you see another thing about it, by which they praise God. There is nothing in the world more beautiful than the different colors that God has given to the dress, or feathers or plumage, of the birds. Some are as white as snow; some as black as coal; some are yellow, some green, some red, some blue, some purple, some the color of gold, and some of silver; while some have nearly all these colors blending together. Look at the peacock, with its splendid tail spread out; or at the humming-bird as it glitters like a living jewel in the sunbeams; or at the bird of Paradise, with all its rich variety of colors, — and it is impossible to think of any thing more beautiful. The flowers of the garden are not more wonderful in the beauty and variety of their colors than the birds of the air are in their dress. And when we think how warm, how water-proof, and yet how beautiful the clothing is which God has prepared for them, we may well say that the birds praise God by the way they dress.

But, in the third place, the birds praise God by THE WAY THEY SING.

Nothing about the birds is more wonderful

than their voices.   When we look at the canary bird, at the nightingale, or the lark of England, or at the mocking-bird of our own country; when we see how small their bodies are,
and especially what tiny little things their
throats are, — we are astonished to see how large
a volume of loud full sound they pour forth.
And if you watch their little throats, rising and
falling and swelling as they fill the air all
round with their sweet music, you cannot help
feeling how good God is to send so many sweet
singers to live in our groves and forests, and
give us such delightful songs!   Suppose the
birds were made without the power of singing,
what a change that would make in the country
everywhere! Then the woods and forests would
be silent.   There would be no music there to
delight our hearts.   What a loss this would be
to us! More than half the joy and pleasure
that we now find from being in the country
would be taken away.   For when we walk
forth through the fields or woods in the morning now, one of the sweetest things that we
find there is the music of the birds as "they

sing among the branches." And so every time
that they open their little throats and pour
forth their delightful songs, it may well be said
that the birds praise God by the way they
sing.

*The fourth way in which the birds praise
God is by* — THE WAY THEY TEACH.

The birds are charming teachers. They set
us good examples in many things ; and, if we only
watch their examples carefully, we shall find
them teaching us some most excellent lessons.

They teach us *the lesson of perseverance.*

When they begin to build their nests, no
matter how much trouble they find in getting
the needed materials, they never give it up, but
go on perseveringly till the work is finished.
And when this is done, and the pretty little
eggs are laid in it, what a picture of patience
and perseverance the mother bird is as she
quietly sits there, day after day, and week after
week, till the eggs are hatched and the young
birds make their appearance !

And then in many other ways the birds set
us an example of perseverance which it will be

very useful for us to follow. A very remarkable case of this kind is mentioned by the Rev. J. W. Turner, of Great Barrington, Mass. He owned the bird spoken of, and published the account over his own name several years ago. This gentleman had a young bobolink which he kept in a cage by itself, near another cage in which were two canary birds. For several months the bobolink never sang any, though he seemed to listen with great pleasure to the song of the canaries. At last he was put into the same cage with them. Then he began to try and learn their song. At first he failed in all his efforts, but he did not give up. He was a good member of " the try company," and he seemed to have great faith in the old proverb that " perseverance conquers all things." He would stand and watch the canaries with the greatest possible attention, and then try to imitate their notes. He would swell out his throat and stretch up his neck as they did, and then, with a great effort, would try to make the same clear sound as they did; but, instead of this, he would only make a miserable squeak.

This made him angry, and he would fly at the canaries and peck them, just as if it was their fault that he could not sing any better. The bobolink ought to have been ashamed of himself for this, and I hope we shall none of us follow this part of his example. But though he got angry he did not give up trying. He seemed determined to succeed, and kept on trying every day for three or four weeks. At length he was able to sound just one note exactly like the canaries. This seemed to encourage him : he kept on for six weeks longer, taking lessons from his teachers every day, till at last he learned the whole song of the canaries, and could sing it as well as they did. Then he would sing with them in perfect harmony and perfect time, always closing at the very same note with them.

And it is singular that although, while he was learning from the canaries, the bobolink would never begin to sing till they struck the key-note; yet, as soon as he felt that he was master of the situation, and knew the song as well as they did, he made himself leader of the choir at once. *He* would always give the signal by a curious sort of *cluck*, as much as to say, "Ready." This was not very amiable in him, but it was very generous in the canaries to forget how he used to peck them, and then to humor him by letting him have his own way.

While he was trying so hard to learn the canary song, he almost forgot his own native music. Then he went back to practise this till he was perfect in it again, and he never rested till he could sing bobolink or canary, or pass from one to the other just as he wanted to do. And thus we see that one of the lessons the birds teach us is the lesson of perseverance.

Another lesson which the birds teach us by their example is the lesson of kindness.

God wants us all to learn this lesson. He tells us to "be kind one to another." Many stories may be told to show how very kind the birds are to each other when they are in trouble. If one wolf, in a pack of wolves, is wounded, the rest will all turn round on him, tear him to pieces, and devour him. And so, if one porpoise, in a school of porpoises, is wounded, the rest will not leave him till they have eaten him up. But it is very different with the birds. If one bird, in a flock of plovers, for instance, is knocked down and wounded, instead of pecking it to pieces, or flying away and leaving it to itself, the rest of the flock will come back and gather round their wounded companion, and will even allow themselves to be taken rather than forsake him in his trouble. This is true kindness.

A young lady once was sitting in a room, near a barn-yard, where a number of chickens and ducks and geese were kept. She was surprised to see a drake come waddling into the room. He came up to her, took hold of the bottom of her dress with his beak, and pulled it towards the door. She pushed him away with her hand. But he came back, and pulled away again as before. She was surprised at this strange conduct, and concluded to follow the drake, and see where he would take her to. When he saw that she was coming, he let go her dress, and waddled on before her. Every little while, he would turn round and see that

she was following, and then keep on. By and
by, he led her to the side of a pond. There she
found a duck, caught by its head in the opening
of a sluice. The drake finding his friend in
distress, and that *he* could not relieve her, had
done the best thing he could to get help for her,
and he succeeded. For the lady took hold of
the poor duck, and soon got her out of her
trouble; and then they waddled off together,
beating their wings, and crying quack-quack-
quack, as if to show how glad and thankful
they were.

There was a little boy once who used to get
his living by selling white sand. A little girl
named Eva, at one of the houses where he sold
his sand, often spoke kindly to him, and sometimes gave him an apple or a cake. One day
the sand boy brought a canary bird, in a tiny
basket cage, to this little girl, to show how
thankful he was for her kindness. Eva was
perfectly delighted with the little bird. She
hung the cage up by the window, and said the
bird was all her own. I am sorry to say that
she would not let her poor little lame sister

6

come near it, or have any thing to do with it. This was very wrong, and the little bird himself made her feel it to be so, as we shall see presently. Eva used sometimes to get fits of the sulks, but her mother shamed her out of them, by showing her how cheerfully the little bird sang out his merry songs every day, no matter what might happen.

And then she made use of the canary, to teach her child a lesson of obedience too. If he happened to be singing loudly, when they wanted him to be quiet, they used to tell him to stop by throwing a towel over the cage. The moment this was done, though he might be just in the midst of a song, he would stop at once. This was a very useful lesson to Eva, and she got into the way of calling the canary her " little preacher." But there was another lesson she was to learn from him, still more important.

Her aunt had a canary which had suddenly gone blind, and they did not know what to do with him, as he was not able to tell where his food was, and so was likely to starve. Eva proposed to her aunt to bring the blind canary,

and put it in the same cage with hers. " I dare
say that Jack " — as she called her bird — " will
help his poor blind friend." So the blind bird
was brought. As Eva put him into her cage,
she made a little speech to Jack, and said:
" Jack, you know you are my little bird preacher.
Preachers ought always to be good ; so I want
you to be very kind to your poor blind play-
mate. And, if he is not very good and patient
in his affliction, you must put up with it, and
preach to him a little occasionally."

Jack did not understand much of what his
mistress said ; and when the blind stranger was
put into his cage, for the first day or two, he
looked very shy at Bill, — as the blind bird was
named, — and kept away from him. But after
a while he seemed to feel a pity for him. He
came near to poor Bill, and showed where the
cup was, which had the seed in it. Then he
would pick up the grains, and put them into
Bill's mouth. Then Bill would clap his wings
and sing a little. After this, Jack led him to
the water cup, and he took a nice bath, and
then they both sang together for a long time, as

merrily as could be. After this, Jack seemed to understand what he was expected to do, and he took charge of poor blind Bill, with as much kindness as a mother would take charge of a sick child.

When Eva saw this, it made her feel very badly. As she was watching the birds one day, her eyes filled with tears, and she said: "Oh, how wicked and impatient I have been to my poor lame sister! I've not been half as good to her as Jack is to poor blind Bill. I hope I shall never speak cross to her again. O Jack! you don't know what a dear good little preacher you have been to me." Then she went to her sister, and threw both arms round her neck, and asked her to forgive her, for ever having been cross to her. Eva never forgot the lesson which her little "bird preacher" had taught her. And when we hear, or read, of things like these that the birds do, we see how nicely they teach us the lesson of kindness.

They also teach us another lesson, and that is the lesson of usefulness.

There are many ways in which the birds

make themselves useful.   You know how useful scavengers, or street cleaners, are in our streets. They remove a great many things which are unpleasant to see, and which, if not taken away, would turn to decay, and have a bad effect upon the air, by making it unhealthy ; and some birds act like scavengers.   In warm countries, great harm would be done if the bodies of dead animals were left to rot in the sun.   But almost the very moment that they fall to the earth, the vultures appear in flocks, and very soon the flesh is all eaten up, and the bones are left picked entirely clean.

Another way in which birds make themselves useful is by destroying worms and insects. These swarm about our gardens and fields, and devour the plants, and grain, and fruit.   If it were not for what the birds do, in thinning off their numbers, it would hardly be possible for the farmers to succeed in raising any thing.

And then we often find examples of birds going out of the way of what seems natural to them, in order to do good and make themselves useful.

In South America they have a bird called the
trumpet-bird, which is very useful. They
train it, as we train our dogs. It will lead the
sheep and cattle out to pasture; keep watch
over them while they are feeding; and bring
them safely home again, at the close of the
day.

In Germany, an aged blind woman used to
be led to church every Sunday by a gander.
He would take hold of her gown, and lead her
along by holding it in his beak. He would
take her to the door of the pew where she sat.
As soon as she was in her place, he would walk
quietly out of the church, and occupy himself
in the church-yard feeding on the grass, till the
service was over, and he heard the people coming out of church. Then he would go to the
pew of his old mistress, and lead her home
again. One day the minister of the church
called to see this old person at her own house.
He found that she had gone out, and he expressed his surprise to her daughter that they
should let her go out alone. "O sir!" replied
the daughter, "there is nothing to fear, mother

is not alone : the gander is with her." Surely
that bird was setting an example of usefulness.

A gentleman in England who lived in the
country had his attention called to a thicket of
bushes near his house one day. He saw a number of birds there, whose loud cries and strange
movements he could not understand. He felt
very curious to find out the meaning of it, so
he crept close up to them, and examined the
bushes. There he found a female bird, whose
wing was caught in such a manner that she
could not get away. Near by was her nest,
containing several young birds. As she was
kept a prisoner there, she was unable to get any
food, either for herself or her young ones. He
stood still, at a little distance, and watched what
was going on. He saw a number of old birds
come flying into the bush, bringing worms and
insects in their mouths, which they gave first to
the mother, and then to her young ones. She
cheered them in their good work with a song
of gratitude. After watching this interesting
sight till his curiosity was satisfied, the gentleman then released the poor bird from her

confinement. In a moment, she flew to her
nest, with a merry song to her deliverer. And
her kind neighbors, who had come to help her,
flew away to their own homes, as soon as they
saw that she did not need their help any more,
singing as they went a song of joy.

How beautiful this was! What real good
neighbors those birds were to their friend in
her distress! And what an example those birds
set us, to try and make ourselves useful by being kind to those who are in trouble, and doing
all we can to help them!

I have only one other story to tell, about the
way in which the birds set us an example of
usefulness.

Two men were neighbors to each other. They
were wood-cutters, and went every day into the
forest to cut wood. They both had children
whom they loved very much, and they were
willing to work hard, so as to supply them with
daily food. One of these men was bright and
cheerful, and was always hoping for the best.
The other was gloomy and fearful. He was
always regretting that he was so poor, and fear-

ing that something would happen to him, so that he would not be able to work, and that then his children would starve. " Oh," he would often say, " how hard it is to be so poor ! If I should get sick, what will become of my wife and children ? "

"Don't be afraid," his cheerful neighbor would say to him : "if you should get sick, God will take care of your family."

One day, as they were going through the forest to their work, they found two bird's-nests in a high tree, and saw that the parent birds were sitting on their eggs. The men watched these nests, day after day as they went past, till they heard the young birds in the nests crying "peep-peep." Each morning as they went by, they saw the mother-birds busily engaged in feeding their young, and they expected soon to see the little ones get strong enough to leave their nests and take care of themselves.

One morning, as the gloomy man was going past this spot by himself, he saw one of the mother-birds going towards her nest, with some food in her mouth for her little ones. Just at

that moment, a hawk darted down on the poor
bird, and bore her away in his claws to make a
breakfast of her.

"Poor bird!" cried the wood-cutter, "what
will become of your young ones now? They
have lost their mother, and they will be left to
die with hunger. And so it will be with my
poor children if any thing should happen to
me."

He was thinking about this all day. It
made him feel so sad that in the evening he
went home another way, because he did not
want to hear the cry of the poor perishing
little ones. The next morning, however, he
concluded to go and look into the nest, and
bury the poor motherless birds, for he was sure
they would be all dead. So he went slowly on;
and when he came to the tree, he was just
going to climb up, when he saw the other
mother-bird going to the nest that had the
orphans in it. Their little heads were lifted
up; their little mouths were open; and their
kind neighbor was acting the part of a mother
to them, and feeding them, just as she fed her

own. He stopped for some time, and watched her, with great interest, as she went and came, taking as much care of the orphan little ones as she did of her own. Just then his cheerful neighbor came along, and he told him, in great surprise, all that had taken place.

"Ah! didn't I tell you so?" said this good man. "And if God takes care of the birds in this way, may we not trust him to take care of us? Don't be afraid any more. If you are taken sick, I will take care of your wife and little ones, just as this kind mother-bird is taking care of her neighbor's orphans. If I get sick, I am sure you will do the same for me. And if any thing should happen to us both, we may be sure that God will take care of our families in some other way."

And so we see how the birds praise God by the way they teach. They teach us the lesson of perseverance, the lesson of kindness, and the lesson of usefulness.

Thus we have spoken of four ways in which the birds praise God. The first is by *the way they live;* the second by *the way they dress;*

the third by *the way they sing ;* and the fourth *by the way they teach.* Let us be thankful for the lessons the birds teach us. Let us try to remember and practise these lessons. And let us always be kind to the birds. Never let us throw stones at them, or rob their nests, or do any thing to frighten or worry them. They are God's creatures, and God wants us to be kind to all his creatures, as he is kind to us.

"Behold the fowls of the air."

IV.

THE DAY-SPRING'S VISIT.

"The Dayspring's Visit." — PAGE 112.

IV.

THE DAY-SPRING'S VISIT.

" The day-spring from on high hath visited us." — LUKE i. 78.

THESE words are in the song that Zacharias, the father of John the Baptist, wrote, in the gladness of his heart, when his son was born according to the saying of the angel Gabriel.

After speaking of the birth of his son John, he goes on to speak of the coming of Christ, whose forerunner John was to be. He calls him "The day-spring from on high, who hath visited us." The word "day-spring" means the beginning of the morning. This is a very proper way to speak of the birth of Christ, or of his coming into our world. The prophet Malachi compares Christ to "the sun of righteousness;" and his birth into our world to the rising of this sun (Mal. iv. 2). The apostle Peter compares him to "*the day-star*" (2 Pet. i. 19). And in the book of Revelation he is called "the bright and morning star" (ch. xxii. 16). And it is a very beautiful comparison which Zacharias uses, when he likens Christ's coming into our world to the visit of the day-spring, or to the dawning of the morning. Before the morning dawns, or the day-spring visits us, as the prophet says, "darkness covers the earth, and gross darkness the people" (Is. lx. 2). But when the morning comes, it drives that darkness away. And it is just the same with our souls till Jesus comes into them. This is spoken of in the hymn which says : —

> " Ashamed of Jesus ! sooner far
> Let night disown each radiant star ;
> 'Tis midnight with my soul till he,
> Bright morning star, bid darkness flee."

And when Christmas comes, and we sing our glad hymns and songs over its return, we are only following the example of the angels, when they raised their song of praise over the birth of Christ, and made the heavens ring with the shout : —

> " Glory to God in the highest ;
> And on earth peace ; good will towards men."

Now, there are four things that always attend

"the day-spring's visit," or the coming of the morning; and when Jesus came into our world he brought these four things; and when he comes into our souls he brings them there too.

The first thing that the visit of the day-spring brings with it is — LIGHT.

In the very next verse, Zacharias goes on to show that this would be the effect of Christ's coming into the world. The object of that coming will be "to *give light* to them that sit in darkness and the shadow of death."

It is when the prophet Isaiah is looking forward to his coming into our world, that he breaks out in this earnest appeal to the church: "Arise, shine! for thy *light* is come, and the glory of the Lord is risen upon thee!" (Is. lx. 1). When foretelling the effect of his birth, he says: "The people that sat in darkness have seen a *great light:* they that dwell in the land of the shadow of death, upon them hath the light shined" (Is. ix. 2). When Christ came into the world he brought light into it; and it is so still wherever he comes with his gospel. This was what he meant when he said: "I am

7

the light of the world: he that followeth me shall not walk in darkness, but shall have the *light of life*" (John viii. 12).

But when Jesus gives us the light that he brings, it is not that we should keep it all for ourselves; we should let it shine for the benefit and blessing of others. This was what he meant when he said: " Let your light so shine before men, that they may see your good works, and glorify your Father who is in heaven" (St. Mark v. 16). And this was what St. Paul meant when he said to the Ephesians: " Now are ye light in the Lord: walk as children of light." (Ephes. v. 8). The business of those who are children of light is to scatter the light around them. There are two ways of doing this. One is by *our example*.

PREACHING BY EXAMPLE.

A Christian man, who lived six miles from the church he attended, complained to his minister one day of the distance he had to walk to church. " Never mind," said the minister, " remember that every Sunday you preach a sermon six miles long: you preach the gospel to all the people you pass on your way to church."

A LIVING BIBLE.

A young man joined one of our churches lately, whose story is worth telling. He was an intelligent, educated young man, and the son of pious parents; but, through some strange influence, he got away from the teaching of his parents, and lost his faith in the Bible and in religion. He became an infidel, and would not allow any one to speak to him on this subject. He gave up going to church. He would not read the printed Bible, and so God sent him a *living* Bible which he could not help reading.

In his father's house a young lady resided, who was a relative of the family. Her fretful and ugly temper made all around her uncomfortable. She was sent to a boarding-school, and was absent some time. While there she became a true and earnest Christian. On her return she was so changed, that all who knew her wondered, and rejoiced. She was patient and cheerful, kind, unselfish, and charitable.

The lips that used to be always uttering cross and bitter words, now spoke nothing but sweet, gentle, loving words. Her presence brought only sunshine, instead of clouds.

Her infidel cousin, George, was greatly surprised at this. He watched her closely for some time, till he became thoroughly satisfied that it was a real change, that had taken place in his young cousin. Then he asked her what had caused this great change.

She told him it was the grace of God, which had made her a Christian, and had changed her heart. He said to himself: " I don't believe that God had any thing to do with it, though she thinks he had. But it is a wonderful change which has taken place in her, and I should like to be as good and amiable as she is. I *will* be so. But I don't want God's help. I'll do it myself."

Then he formed a set of good resolutions. He tried to control his tongue and his temper, and kept a strict watch over himself. But it seemed to do no good. He was all the time doing, and saying, what he did not wish to do and say. And as he failed, time after time, he would turn and study his good cousin's example. He would read this living Bible, and say to himself: "How does it happen that she, who has not so much knowledge, or as much strength of character as I have, can do what I can't do. She must have some help that I don't know of. It must be, as she says, the help of God. I will seek that help! He went into his chamber, and prayed to that God whose very existence he had denied. He prayed earnestly. God heard him and helped him, and he became a Christian. That young lady received light from Jesus, and then she let it shine. And the shining of that light brought her cousin out of the darkness of infidelity. One way in which we can scatter the light is *by example.*

The other way in which we can do this *is by helping to send the gospel to those who are in darkness.*

SOWING LIGHT.

A blind girl came to her minister and gave him five dollars for the missionary cause.

He was surprised at the greatness of the

amount, and said : " My friend, you are blind ; and you have to work for your own living, I think this is too much for you to give."

" It is true, sir, that I am blind," she said ; " but I can prove to you that I can spare this money better than those who see."

" Pray tell me how that is ? " said the minister.

" I am a basket-maker," answered the girl ; " and as I am blind, I can make my baskets as easily in the dark as with a light. Other girls have, during the last winter, spent more than that amount for light to work by. I had no such expense, and so I can spare this money to help in sending the Bible to the heathen." And, in either or both of these two ways, we may help to spread the light.

The first thing that the day-spring brings with it is the light.

But, in addition to light, — BEAUTY — *attends the day-spring when it comes.*

How much beauty there is in the colors that appear in the sky, and in the clouds, when the sun is rising, and the day-spring appearing !

Crimson, and purple, and gold, and other beautiful colors, are all blending together, as if in honor of the day-spring's coming. And then, not in the sky only, but wherever the beams of the morning are shining beauty appears. The mists that float over the plains are beautiful. The dark shadows stretching out here, and there, are beautiful. The mountains, the hills, the rocks, the trees, the fields, are all beautiful, as the day-spring's light is poured around them.

And when Jesus, "the day-spring from on high," visited our world, he brought beauty with him, and spread it around him everywhere. The prophet Isaiah said of him, that he would "give beauty for ashes; the oil of joy for mourning; and the garment of praise for the spirit of heaviness" (Isa. lxi. 3). He was spreading beauty around him by the miracles he performed every day. When he healed the sick, and raised the dead; when he made the lame to walk, and the blind to see, and the deaf to hear, and the dumb to speak,—he was really giving beauty for ashes.

And by the lessons that he taught, as well as

by the miracles he performed, he was doing the same thing. Those lessons taught men how to get their sins pardoned, and their hearts changed, and their lives made useful, and good, and pure, and holy. And these are among the most beautiful things that we know. And this is what Jesus is doing still, for those who receive his teachings. When he comes into the souls of his people, he comes to make them beautiful, because he comes to make them like himself. When we come to see Jesus as "the King in his beauty" in heaven, we shall feel that there never was a face so beautiful as his. And if we learn to know and love Jesus, and to become daily more like him, it will make our characters, and all about us beautiful. Here are some lines which carry out this idea. They are about

BEAUTIFUL THINGS.

Beautiful faces are those that wear,
It matters little if dark or fair,
Whole-souled honesty printed there.

Beautiful eyes are those that show,
Like crystal panes where hearth-fires glow,
Beautiful thoughts that burn below.

Beautiful lips are those whose words
Leap from the heart like songs of birds,
Yet whose utterance prudence girds.

Beautiful hands are those that do
Work that is earnest, and brave, and true,
Moment by moment, the long day through.

Beautiful feet are those that go
On kindly ministries to and fro,
Down lowliest ways, if God wills it so.

Beautiful shoulders are those that bear
Ceaseless burdens of homely care
With patient grace, and daily prayer.

Beautiful lives are those that bless,
Silent rivers of happiness,
Whose hidden fountains but few can guess.

Beautiful twilight, at set of sun ;
Beautiful goal, with race well run ;
Beautiful rest, with work well done.

Beautiful graves, where grasses creep,
Where brown leaves fall, where drifts lie deep,
Over worn-out hands : oh, *beautiful sleep !*

Here is an illustration or two, of the way
in which Jesus helps those who love and serve
him, to make their lives beautiful.

HOW TO GET RID OF A BAD TEMPER.

A lady, who was the head of a family, was very much worried and disturbed by a bad temper. She had a good Christian girl, who had become a servant in the household. One day she spoke very crossly to this servant, when there was no occasion for it. Then she made an apology to her, for the bad temper she had shown, and expressed the hope that nothing like it would ever take place again.

"O ma'am!" said the servant, "I pity you very much. I once had just such a temper as yours, and I can feel for you."

"Why I should have thought that nothing ever troubled you in this way, and yet you say you had just such a temper as I have. Pray tell me what you did with it?"

"I took it to Jesus. I gave it to him, and took him as my Saviour. He took away my bad temper, and taught me to be like him."

"Oh, how I wish he would take away my temper, and teach me to be like him!"

"He will, mistress, if you bring it to him,

and ask him earnestly to take it away. It is too strong for you to overcome it ; but he can teach you to do it, and he will if you ask him."

Then the mistress and the maid knelt down together, and the maid prayed for the mistress. She prayed that Jesus would give her the help of his grace, to change her bad temper, and make her meek and gentle and kind and loving. And Jesus heard that prayer. The temper of that Christian lady was changed. The mistress and the maid both had the same mind, or temper, that was in Christ Jesus. And to have two gentle, loving tempers there, added wonderfully to the comfort and the beauty of that home.

A LITTLE THING, BUT VERY BEAUTIFUL.

A gentleman, whose name was Harvy, was riding slowly on horseback, along a dusty road. As he did so, he was looking about in every direction for a stream, or for a house, from the well of which he might refresh his tired, and thirsty horse, with a good drink of water. While doing this, he turned a bend in the road, and saw before him a comfortable-looking farm-house; and at the same time a boy, ten or twelve years old, came out into the road with a pail of water, and stood directly before him.

"What do you wish, my boy?" said Mr. Harvy, stopping his horse.

"Would your horse like a drink, sir?" said the boy, respectfully.

"Indeed he would, and I was just wondering where I could get it."

Mr. Harvy thought, of course, that the boy was in the habit of doing this to earn a few pennies; and so, when his horse had taken his drink, he offered the boy a bit of silver, and was very much surprised to see him refuse it.

"I wish you would take it, my little man," said he, as he looked earnestly at the child, and noticed, for the first time, that he was lame.

"Indeed, sir, I don't want it. It is little enough that I can do for myself, or any one else. I am lame, and my back is bad, sir; but mother says no matter how small a favor may seem, if it is all we can do, God loves it as much as he does a larger favor; and this is the most that I can do for others. You see, sir, it is eight miles from here to the next village, and I happen to know that there is no stream crossing the road in all that distance; and so, sir, almost every one passing here is sure to have a thirsty horse, and I try to do a little good by giving the poor creatures a drink."

Mr. Harvy looked with great interest on the boy. He thanked him for his kindness; and, as he went on his way, he felt that the little fellow had preached him a sermon that he would not soon forget.

How beautiful this was! That was a little Christian boy, trying to follow the example of the loving Saviour, who "went about doing good." And, even in that lonely place in the country, he managed to find a way in which he could make himself useful.

And if we have the spirit of this boy, and try to do all the good we can, we may all find something to do. We shall find all about us, not thirsty animals only, but thirsty souls, and we shall be able to lead them to Jesus, the fountain of living water, that they may drink of the water that he gives, and live for ever.

Let us try to follow the example of this little boy, and then, in the good that is done, we shall see beauty all around us, — the beauty that follows from the day-spring's visit.

The third thing that follows when the day-spring appears is — JOY.

This is what David teaches, when he says: "Joy cometh in the morning" (Ps. xxx. 5). If we are well and happy, the morning is sure to bring us joy. Go out into the fields about sunrise, on a summer morning, and listen. How sweet the sounds you hear! The birds have begun their morning songs of praise. How charming to listen to the notes they sing! And every sound you hear seems to tell of gladness. The day-spring has visited us. Morning has come once more, and "joy cometh in the morning." The prophet Isaiah speaks of Christ as "appearing to the joy of his people" Isa. lxvi. 5.

It was so, when he first appeared. When the angel came to tell of his birth, he said to the shepherds of Bethlehem: "Behold, I bring you good tidings of *great joy*, which shall be to all people ! (St. Luke ii. 10).   And it is this thought which makes Christmas so bright and happy a season to us.   We think of Christ's coming into our world.   We think of all the blessings he brought with him when he came, and it fills us with joy and gladness.

He did bring joy into the world when he first entered it.   And now, when he comes into any heart, any home, any neighborhood, he always brings joy with him.   The day-spring's coming causes joy in two ways: the first is by *what he does for us*; the second, *by what he helps us to do for others*.

How much Jesus does for us which causes joy !

HER INIQUITY IS PARDONED.

A little girl, ten years old, had been very much troubled about her sins.   Her mother told her that Jesus pardons all who are really sorry for their sins, and ask him to forgive them.   When the child understood this sweet truth, she confessed her sins to Jesus, and asked him to forgive them.   She believed his promise to do so, and this made her wonderfully happy. " O mother ! " she said, " if all the world only knew this ! I wish I could tell everybody. Do let me run and tell some of the neighbors, that they may love Jesus, and be as happy as I am."

" Ah, my child ! I'm afraid they would only laugh at you," said her mother.

" O mother ! I think they would believe me : do let me run over to the shoemaker across the way, and tell him about it."

She ran over, and began by telling him that he must die, and that he was a sinner, and that she was a sinner too, but that her blessed Saviour had forgiven her sins, and now she was so happy that she knew not how to tell it. The shoemaker was struck with surprise. He had never paid any attention to these things. But now he began earnestly to pray for pardon. It ended in his becoming a Christian. When he felt the joy of pardon, he spoke of it to his friends. And so, by trying to share her joy with the old shoemaker, that little girl was the means of bringing a number of persons in that neighborhood to Jesus. And they all felt the joy which the day-spring's visit occasions.

A GOOD ILLUSTRATION OF THE CHRISTIAN'S JOY.

There is a story of Mithridates, a celebrated king in Asia, which illustrates this part of our subject very well. This king became interested in an old musician, who had taken part in the music performed at a feast in the royal palace. On awaking one morning, this old man saw the tables in his house covered with vessels of silver and gold; a number of servants were standing by, who offered him rich garments to put on, and told him there was a horse standing at the door for his use, whenever he might wish to ride. The old man thought it was only a dream he was having. But the servants said it was no dream at all. It was a reality. What is the meaning of it? asked the astonished old man. "It means this," said the servants: "the king has determined to make you a rich man at once. And these things that you see are only a small part of what he has given you. So please use them as your own."

At last he believed what they told him. Then

8

he put on the purple robe, and mounted the horse; and as he rode along, he kept saying to himself,— "All these are mine! All these are mine!"

Of course that old man would have great joy. What the king had given him would make him happy. But this was nothing to what Jesus gives to all those who love and serve him. He not only makes us rich, but he says we shall be kings and priests — for ever! (Rev. i. 6). No one can tell all that is meant by this promise. But we know it is something better than any earthly king has ever had. For Jesus says, that these "kings and priests" "shall *inherit all things*" (Rev. xxi. 7). And so we may well say that *what Jesus does for us*, when we become his people, is enough to give us joy.

And then he gives us joy, too, by *what he helps us to do for others.* There is no joy in the world like that we feel in trying to do good to others. Jesus expects all his people to do this. And, if we try to do it, we shall know something about the joy which follows from the day-spring's visit. Here is a nice illustration of this. We may call it

A LITTLE ERRAND FOR GOD.

Helen stood on the door-step, with a tiny basket in her hand. While she was standing there, her father drove up in a carriage, and said: "I'm glad to see you are all ready to go out, my darling; I'm come to take you to Mr. Lee's park, to see his new deer."

"O, thank you, papa! but I can't go just now. The deer will keep, and we can go to-morrow. I've got a very particular errand that I must attend to at this time," said the little girl.

"What is it, dear?" asked her father.

"Oh! it's to carry *this* somewhere," and she held up the little basket.

Her father smiled, and asked: "Who is the errand for, my child?"

"For my own self, papa; but—oh, no! I guess not. It's a little errand for God, papa."

"Well, I will not hinder you, my little dear," said the good father, tenderly. "But can I help you any?"

"No, sir; I was going to carry my big orange, that I saved from dinner, to old Peter."

" Is old Peter sick ? "

" No, I hope not : but he never has any thing nice ; and he's so good and thankful ! Big folks only give him cold meat and broken bread ; and I thought an orange would look nice on his table, and make him so happy ! Don't you think poor well folks ought to be comforted sometimes, as well as poor sick folks, papa ? "

" Yes, my dear, I do ; and yet, we often forget them till sickness or starvation comes. You are right, my child ; this is a little errand for God.   Get into the buggy, and I will drive you to old Peter's, and wait till you have done your errand, and then we'll go to the park and see the deer.   Have you got a pin, Helen ? "

" Yes, papa ; here's one."

" Well, here is a two-dollar note for you to fix on the skin of the orange. That will pay old Peter's rent for two weeks ; and perhaps this will be a little errand for God, too," said her father.

And little Helen was very happy ; — she was full of joy as her tiny fingers fastened the nice new two-dollar bill to the orange. And as they drove away to the park, her father felt very happy too. That talk with his dear child had done him good like a sermon. And it filled him with joy to think, that one he loved so much, was beginning so early, to tread in the blessed steps of Christ's most holy life.

And so, both by what Jesus does for us, and by what he enables us to do for others, we see how joy follows from the day-spring's visit.

How well we may repeat here, the words of the hymn we sometimes sing : —

> "Joy to the world! the Lord is come!
>   Let earth receive her King;
> Let every heart prepare him room,
>   And heaven and nature sing.
>
> Joy to the world! the Saviour reigns;
>   Let men their songs employ;
> While fields, and floods, rocks, hills, and plains
>   Repeat the sounding joy."

But there is one other thing that always follows when the morning comes, and the day-spring visits us, and that is — ACTIVITY.

During the darkness of the night, work is

generally stopped, and the world is wrapped in sleep and stillness. But, when the morning comes, men wake from their sleep, and go forth to the labors and duties of another day. And so the day-spring, or the morning, when it comes, leads to activity.

Now, it was night in the world before Jesus entered it. And it is night in our souls till Jesus comes into them. But Jesus came, as the day-spring, to waken men out of sleep, and stir them up to activity, in working for their souls and for heaven. When he comes into our souls to dwell there, it is like morning coming after a long night. And great activity follows the day-spring's visit. Then we begin to see what Jesus has done for us. We see his wonderful love, and the thought of that love stirs our hearts and souls to be active in his service.

One of the best illustrations of this activity in good works, following from the day-spring's visit to the soul, is seen in the case of the apostle Paul. The visit of the day-spring was made to him on his way to Damascus. He

was going there to persecute the followers of
Jesus, and put them to death. But just before
he reached Damascus, he had that wonderful
vision of which we read in Acts ix. 1–9.
Then he found out, to his amazement, that
Jesus of Nazareth, whom he was persecuting in
his followers, was really the great Messiah, —
the divine Saviour, who was seated at the right
hand of the throne of God. Then he saw, for
the first time, what Jesus had done for him.
Then his eyes were opened to see the wonderful love of Jesus. *That* was the day-spring's
visit to Saul of Tarsus. And great activity
followed it. He became Paul, the preacher ;
and there never has been a preacher since equal
to him. He felt the love of Christ constrain-
ing, or drawing him to Jesus. It drew his
whole heart and soul to him ; it led him to give
up his life, and all that he had, to the service of
Jesus. And from that time, wonderful indeed
was the activity that marked the life of Paul.
He went all up and down the earth, telling the
marvellous story of Jesus and his love. By
day and by night, in summer and in winter, on

the land and on the sea, he was always at work for Jesus, and for the souls of men. No labor could tire him, no danger could frighten him, and no opposition or persecution could stop him. Through all the years of his long life, this activity continued, and never ceased till he met a martyr's death, and went to dwell for ever with that glorious Saviour whom he had served so faithfully.

After the great apostle St. Paul had found out what a precious Saviour he had in Jesus, the activity he showed was all intended to try and bring other people to Jesus, that they might be made happy too. And when we learn to know and love Jesus ourselves, we should be active in bringing others to him. Let us look at some illustrations of the way in which we may be active for Jesus.

BOB'S SERMON.

Far away out in the mining regions of the great West, a minister of the Methodist church was holding meetings. We may give the account of it in his own words.

"The place," says he, "was a desperate one, and I had been warned not to go there; but God went with me, and took care of me. I found an organized band of gamblers, who had been the terror of all preachers, and all good people in that neighborhood. The leader of this band was known as Bob. Through the favor of God's wonderful Providence, I got on the right side of Bob; and by a little management, I gained the confidence of the whole band. They came to church, and behaved with the greatest propriety while there.

"After a while, Bob became interested in the subject of religion, and, before long, he expressed a desire to be baptized and to join the church. Thus the day-spring visited his soul, and it made him anxious and active to have his friends become Christians too. At one of our meetings he and his band were present. When I was about to give out a hymn, Bob rose, and said: —

"'Parson, may I say a few words to the boys?'

"'Say on, Bob,' I replied.

"Turning round to his companions, and looking the one nearest to him straight in the face, he said : —

"'Harry, my boy, you know I love you. You and I have been together on many a spree. Harry, old fellow, I can't turn away from you. I can't throw you off; but Harry, I don't want to go the old road any more. I'm down, clean down to the bed-rock. Boys, you all know me; I don't want to quit you: but come, let's all 'bout face. I tell you, boys, we are all gone up the flume, if we keep on the way we've been living. I'm going to try t' other road, boys; come, go with me, won't you ?'

"With such words as these, only with much more of the strange phrases which the miners use, he went on begging his companions to come to Christ. The effect of Bob's speech was very great. The whole band melted down under it. Then we had a time of weeping and confessions. Strange stories were told about early homes forsaken, and about early lessons long forgotten; and about how they had gone down, down in the ways of sin and misery."

Then there were prayers offered for them,

instructions given to them, and finally a large part of the band became Christians and joined the church. And this was all the result of God's blessing on the active efforts that Bob made, after the day-spring had visited his own soul, to save the souls of his old companions in sin.

A LITTLE GIRL BRINGING FIVE PERSONS TO CHRIST.

A minister of the gospel was speaking one day to a little girl who attended his church. She was about eight years of age. "Well, Ettie," he said, "suppose the Lord Jesus were to come to-night, where would you be?"

"I should be with him, sure," was her answer.

"How do you know that?" he asked.

"Why, because he loves me," was her quick reply. "The Bible says he died for all; and, therefore, he must have died for me."

He then asked :—

"Are you not afraid to die, Ettie?"

"Oh, no!" she said, "Jesus put away my sins; and, when he died, he took a thief with him."

" If Jesus took the thief with him, whom are you going to take ? "

She said: " I've got five to go with me."

" What do you mean ? " asked the minister.

" I've got my little brother Charley, and my aunt Susan, and my cousins, Neddy and Willie and Freddie, all ready to go with me to Jesus."

When this little girl found that the dayspring had visited her soul, and that Jesus had washed away her sins, she was so full of joy that she could not go to sleep. Her brother Charley said to her : " Why don't you go to sleep, Ettie ? "

" Oh, I've got something, Charley, that makes me so happy, I can't go to sleep ; and, if you had it, you would not be able to sleep either ! "

" What have you got? " asked Charley.

" I've got eternal life. Jesus has washed my sins away, and made me ready for heaven. Won't you come to him, Charley, and have your sins washed away, and get eternal life ? "

Charley listened to his sister's words, and said he would like to be a Christian too, and have eternal life.

Then Ettie sat down and wrote to her aunt Susan, and told her how happy she was in trying to love and serve the blessed Saviour, and asked her if she didn't want to have Jesus make her happy too. This led her aunt, for the first time in her life, to begin seriously to think about these things. And very soon she became a Christian. And so, in the first efforts of her activity, after the day-spring had visited her own soul, we see how little Ettie had been the means of bringing five persons to Jesus.

ROOM FOR ALL TO WORK HERE.

"What have my class done for Jesus since we last met?" asked the teacher of a large infant class, one Sunday morning.

One said: "I earned some money for the heathen, by doing errands;" another said: "I minded the sick baby, to help mother;" another: "I fetched hump-back Billy to school, though the boys laughed at me." And so, one after another, told in a half-bashful, half-pleasant way, of the little activities of the week, the different things they had tried to do, to show their love for the day-spring's visit, which had come to them in the clear teachings of their faithful teacher.

At last, a little girl named Molly, about four years old, lifted up her hand, and waved it to and fro, to catch the teacher's attention.

" Well, Molly, my dear, and what do you do for Jesus ? "

The little face was flushed with eager interest, as the unexpected reply came : —

" *I scrubs.*"

Some of the children began to laugh ; but the good teacher checked them at once, by saying : " Don't laugh at Molly, my dear children. Her share in the work my class is doing for Jesus is as important as any. If she tries to help her mother, by scrubbing a bench or a table, even though it is not done as well as a grown person could do it, yet she earns the same smile of love as the older ones, who can do errands, and earn money for the missionary box."

" ' She hath done what she could,' is the highest praise that can be spoken of any one ;

and little Molly has done that. Go on, Molly dear, and scrub all you can."

And so we have spoken of the day-spring's visit; and of the four things that attend, or follow it; these are: light, and beauty, and joy, and activity. The day-spring has visited us. Let us be careful that those around us may see in our lives all the light, and beauty, and joy, and activity that should follow from that visit.

V.

THE GOOD SOLDIERS.

"Good Soldiers." — Page 142.

V.

THE GOOD SOLDIERS.

" Good soldiers of Jesus Christ." — 2 TIMOTHY ii. 3.

THERE is a great deal said in the Bible about soldiers. The church of Jesus Christ — made up of all the people who love him — is compared in one place to "an army with banners" (Cant. vi. 4). Our blessed Saviour is spoken of as "the leader, or commander" of this army (Is. lv. 4). And in one place in the New Testament, St. Paul calls Jesus "the Captain of our salvation" (Heb. ii. 10). And, in the verse in which our text is found, he calls on all who are trying to be true Christians to "endure hardness as good soldiers of Jesus Christ."

Now, the one great object we have in view, in our Sunday-school work, is that all our scholars should become Christians. And every true Christian is a soldier of Jesus Christ. Perhaps some of the girls may think: "Well, this subject does not suit us. We do not want to be soldiers." That is true. We do not want our dear daughters, and sisters, to wear swords, and shoulder muskets, and go out to fight for their country in time of war. But then we do want you all to be the "soldiers of Jesus Christ." If you become Christians, this is just what you will be. Some of the best and bravest soldiers that Jesus has ever had, have been female soldiers. And so this subject suits the girls as well as the boys. And now, the question before us is,—*How may we become good soldiers of Jesus Christ?* I wish to speak of three things that are necessary, if we wish to learn this lesson.

In the first place, to become good soldiers of Jesus Christ — WE MUST WEAR THE UNIFORM *of Christ.*

The soldier's uniform is the dress that he wears. This is often very beautiful. Sometimes the uniform is of a blue color; sometimes it is gray, or yellow, or green, or scarlet. Sometimes it is all of one color; while at other times, it is made up of a variety of different colors. To see a whole regiment of men, all dressed in the same uniform, and keeping step together, is a very pleasing sight.

But the uniform which the soldiers of Jesus wear is not the dress that is put upon their bodies, but the dress that is put upon their souls. This uniform is not made up of different-colored cloth, such as we see other soldiers wear. No; but it is made up of the tempers, or dispositions, which form their character.

To wear the uniform of Jesus, then, is to have the same mind, or spirit, or temper that he had. And the Bible tells us that, unless we have the mind or spirit of Jesus, we cannot be his servants or followers.

Now, let us see what sort of a mind or spirit Jesus had, and then we can tell whether we are wearing the uniform of Jesus or not.

The spirit of Jesus was a *gentle* spirit: this is part of the uniform of Jesus; and, if we want to be good soldiers of Jesus, we must wear this uniform. We must try to be gentle.

We never hear that Jesus spoke a cross or angry word. Sometimes he spoke severely to the people about their sins, but he was never cross. The Jews were very unkind to him; they told stories about him. They called him bad names: but he never spoke back to them in the same way; he never threatened them or stormed at them. He came as God's lamb to be sacrificed for us, and he was as gentle and mild as a lamb. And we cannot be good soldiers of Jesus Christ, unless we wear this part of his uniform, and try to be gentle as he was. But, if we do wear this uniform, we shall be very useful.

An old gentleman once lived in a large house. He had plenty of money, and servants, and every thing he wanted, and yet he was not happy; he was not gentle. When things did not just please him he would get cross, and speak sharply. His servants all left him, and he was in great trouble. Quite discouraged, he went to a neighbor's to tell him of his difficulties. This man was "a good soldier of Jesus Christ." He was wearing the uniform of gentleness. After listening to his neighbor's story, he said to him : —

"It seems to me, my friend, it would be well for you to *oil yourself a little.*"

"To oil myself! What do you mean?"

"Let me explain. Some time ago, one of the doors in our house had a creaking hinge. It made such a disagreeable noise whenever it was opened or shut, that nobody cared to touch it. One day I oiled its hinges; and, since then, we have had no trouble with it."

"And so you think I'm like a creaking hinge, do you?" said the neighbor. "Pray, how do you want me to oil myself?"

"It's easy enough to tell that," said his friend. "Go home, and engage a servant. If he does well, praise him for it. If he doesn't do just as you would like, don't get cross, and scold him. Soften your voice and words with the oil of love and gentleness, and you will not have much trouble."

That was good advice. If we are good soldiers of Jesus we must carry this precious oil with us, and use it all the time. Gentleness is part of the uniform of Jesus. Let us try to wear this.

But the spirit of Jesus was *a forgiving spirit.*
This is another part of his uniform that we
must wear if we wish to be good soldiers of Jesus.

Such a spirit of forgiveness as Jesus showed
was never seen in our world before or since.
The Jews persecuted him and put him to death,
in a very cruel way, by nailing him to the
cross, although he had never done any thing
but good to them all his days.   And yet, while
he hung suffering on the cross, Jesus did not
feel angry towards them.   He spoke no harsh,
cross words to them.   But he felt pity for them.
He prayed for them, and said : " Father, forgive
them, for they know not what they do !"   How
wonderful this was !   What a forgiving spirit
Jesus had !   This was the uniform he wore.
And we must wear it too, if we would be " good
soldiers of Jesus Christ."

The superintendent of a Sunday-school was
standing at his window one day.   He saw two
of the girls belonging to his school going by.
They had evidently had a quarrel with some
acquaintance.   One of them was saying to the
other, in a very angry voice : —

"Sallie, I tell you what, if I were in your place I'd never speak to her again. I'd be mad at her as long as I lived."

The superintendent listened very anxiously to hear what Sallie would say to this. He felt greatly relieved when she said : —

"No, Lou, I wouldn't do so for all the world. You know we must try and be like Jesus. I'm going to forgive and forget as soon as I can, and try to make her love me. This is what Jesus would have done."

There you see the uniform of Jesus. That dear girl was a good soldier of Jesus Christ. She had a forgiving spirit.

And then the spirit of Jesus was a *trusting* spirit. He felt sure that his Father was always with him, and would never let any thing hurt him. Even when his enemies had taken him, and were going to crucify him, he said that, if he should ask his Father he would send legions of angels to deliver him out of their hands. And this is just the feeling that he wants us to have. If we are the soldiers of Jesus, and are trying to love and serve him, he will always be with us.

He will watch over us and take care of us, and so we never need be afraid. Let me tell you about a little girl who had this trusting spirit.

She was only four years old, and was called Birdie. She had been taught that God loved her, and always took care of her.

One day there was a heavy thunder-storm, and Birdie's sisters, and even her mamma, laid by their sewing, and drew their chairs into the middle of the room. They were pale and trembling with fear. But Birdie stood close by the window, watching the storm with great interest.

"O, mamma, a'int that bu'ful?" she cried, clapping her hands with delight, as a vivid flash of lightning, burst from the black clouds, and the thunder pealed, and rattled over head.

"It's God's voice, Birdie," said mamma, and her own voice trembled.

"He talks velly loud, don't he, mamma? S'pose it's so as deaf Aunt Betsy can hear, and uver deaf folks."

"O Birdie, dear! come straight away from

that window," said her sister Nellie, whose face
was all white with fear.

"*What for?*" asked Birdie.

"Oh! because the lightning is so sharp, and
it thunders so loud."

But Birdie shook her head, and, looking over
her shoulder with a happy smile on her face,
lisped out : —

"If it funders, let it funder! It's God that
makes it funder, and he'll take care of me. I
ain't a bit afraid to hear God talk, sister Nelly."
That was beautiful : Birdie was a good soldier of
Jesus Christ. She had a trusting spirit. This
is part of the uniform of Jesus. The spirit of
Jesus is a gentle spirit, a forgiving spirit, a
trusting spirit. These help to make up the
uniform of Jesus. The first thing for us to do,
if we would be good soldiers of Jesus is to wear
the uniform of Jesus.

*The second thing for us to do, if we would be
good soldiers of Jesus Christ, is to* — OBEY THE OR-
DERS OF JESUS.

The most important thing for a soldier to do
is to learn to obey. No matter how hard, or

dangerous the thing is that he is told to do, there is no choice left him, but just to go and do it. He may be perfectly sure that he will be killed in trying to do it. That makes no difference. He must obey. It is impossible to be a good soldier without learning this lesson.

Many years ago, the great battle of Waterloo was fought in Europe, between the English and the French. The Duke of Wellington commanded the English army, and the Emperor, Napoleon Bonaparte, commanded the French. In the midst of the battle, the French made a furious attack on a particular part of the English lines. It was very important that the English soldiers should stand their ground then, and hold that point. The success of the battle depended on it. Courier after courier came dashing into the presence of the Duke of Wellington. They asked him to send reinforcements to that part of the field, or to order the troops away from it, or else they would be compelled to retreat from the fierce onsets of the French. By all these messengers the Duke sent back the same order, — " Stand firm."

"We shall all perish," said one of the officers. "Stand firm," was still the Duke's answer. "You'll find us all there, when the battle's over," said the officer, and galloped back to his post to die. And it turned out just as he said. Not one of that gallant brigade left his post. And not one was living when the battle was over. They obeyed their orders. They "stood firm." But they all died in doing it. Those were good soldiers. They had learned to obey orders.

Some time ago, a large ship was going from England to the East Indies. She was carrying a regiment of soldiers. When they were about half way through their voyage, the vessel sprang a leak, and began to fill with water. The life-boats were launched and made ready; but there were not enough of them to save all on board the ship. Only the officers of the ship, the cabin passengers, and some of the crew, could be taken in the boats. The soldiers had to be left on board, to go down with the ship. The officers determined to die with their men. The colonel was afraid the men would get unruly if

they had nothing to do. That he might pre-
vent this he ordered them to prepare for parade.
Soon they all appeared in full dress. He set
the regimental band on the quarter-deck, with
orders to keep on playing lively airs. Then he
formed his men in close ranks on the deck.
With his sword drawn in his hand, he took his
place at their head. Every officer and man is
at his post. The vessel is gradually sinking;
but they stand steady at their post, each man
keeping step. And then, just as the vessel is
settling for its last plunge, and death is rushing
in upon them, the colonel cries, — "Present
arms!" and that whole regiment of brave men
go down into their watery grave, presenting
arms as death approached them.

Those were good soldiers. They had learned
to obey orders. But this is a hard lesson to
learn.

I heard, some time ago, of a German captain,
who found it difficult to teach his men this lesson. He was drilling a company of volunteers.
The parade ground was a field near the seaside.
The men were going through their exercises

very nicely. But the captain thought he would give them a lesson about obeying orders. They were marching up and down, in the line of the water, at some distance from it. He concluded to give them an order to march directly towards the water, and see how far they would go. The men are marching along. "Halt, company!" says the captain. In a moment they halt. "Right face!" is the next word, and instantly they wheel round. "Forwarts, march!" is the next order. At once they begin to march directly towards the water. On they go, nearer and nearer to it. Soon they reach the edge of the water. Then there is a sudden halt. "Vat for you shtop? I no say halt," cried the captain.

"Why, captain, here's the water," said one of the men.

"Vell, vat of it?" cried he, greatly excited. "Vater is notting. Fire is notting. Every ting is notting, ven I say, 'Forwarts, march!' Den you *must* 'forwarts, march.'"

The captain was right. The first duty of a soldier is to learn to obey. If we want to be good soldiers of Jesus, we must learn to obey his orders.

Several boys were playing marbles. In the midst of their sport, it began to rain. One of the boys named Freddie, stopped and said: "Boys, I must go home. Mother told me not to stay out in the rain."

"Your mother — fudge!" said two or three of the boys. "The rain won't hurt you any more than it will us." Freddie turned on them with a look of pity, and yet, with the courage of a hero, while he calmly said: "*I'll not disobey my mother for any of you.*"

That was the spirit of a good soldier.

After a great battle once, the general was talking to his officers about the events of the day. He asked them who had done the best that day. Some spoke of one man who had fought very bravely, and some of another.

"No," said the general, "you are all mistaken. The best man in the field to-day was a soldier who was just lifting up his arms to strike an enemy, but when he heard the trumpet sound a retreat, he checked himself, and dropped his arm, without striking the blow. That perfect and ready obedience to the will of his general, is the noblest thing that has been done to-day."

One of the best illustrations I ever heard of the way in which we ought to learn to obey God, was given once by a negro preacher, when speaking on this point. He said: "Bredren, whatever de good Lord tell me to do in dis blessed book, dat I'm gwine to do. If I see in it dat I must jump froo' a stone wall, I'm gwine to jump. Gettin froo' it 'longs to God. Jumpin at it 'longs to me."

That is the true spirit of a soldier.

And this is the spirit that we must have if we want to be "good soldiers of Jesus Christ."

We must obey the orders of Jesus. This is the second thing for good soldiers of Jesus to do.

But there is a third thing for us to do, in order to be good soldiers of Jesus, we must — FOLLOW THE EXAMPLE OF JESUS.

Jesus came into our world, not only to die for our sins, and to show us by his teaching how we ought to live; but he came to do one other

10

thing. This was a very important thing. He
came to leave us an example that we might
safely follow. The apostle tells us that Jesus
has "left us an example that we should follow
his steps" (1 Peter ii. 21). The example of Jesus
is the only perfect example that we can find.
The best people in the world do wrong some
time; and so, if we follow their example, we
cannot always be sure it is right. But Jesus
never did, or said, or thought, or felt any thing
that was wrong. We can follow his example
safely. We never need have a moment's fear
about going wrong when we are treading in his
steps.

And Jesus wants us to follow his example,
because he knows that example is more powerful than words.

When Alexander the Great was leading his
army over some mountains once, they found
their way all stopped up with ice and snow. His
soldiers were tired out with hard marching,
and so disheartened with the difficulties before
them, that they halted. It seemed as if they
would rather lie down and die than try to go

on any farther. When Alexander saw this, he did not begin to scold the men and storm at them. Instead of this, he got down from his horse, laid aside his cloak, took up a pickaxe, and, without saying a word to any one, went quietly to work, digging away at the ice. As soon as the officers saw this, they did the same. The men looked on in surprise for a few moments, and then, forgetting how tired they were, they went to work with a will, and pretty soon they got through all their difficulties. Those were good soldiers, because they followed the example of their leader.

When the native converts in the island of Madagascar used to come to the missionaries and want to be baptized, it often happened that questions like these would be put to them : " What was it that first led you to think of becoming Christians ? Was it some sermon you heard, or something that was read from the Bible ? "

In many cases the answer would be: " No, it was not any particular sermon, or passage from the Bible ; but it was the example of those who had become Christians, that led us to think seriously about these things. We knew such an one who used to be a thief, another who was a drunkard, and another who was very cruel and unkind to his family. But now they are all changed. The thief has become an honest man, the drunkard is sober and respectable, and the man of bad temper has become gentle and kind in his home. There must be something in a religion that can work such changes as these."

You see that those Madagascar Christians were good soldiers of Jesus. They were following his example. In this way, they were doing more good than even the missionaries did with their preaching.

"I say, Jim," said Harry to his brother; "didn't you feel mad, at noon to-day, when mother kept us waiting half-an-hour for our dinner?"

"Well, Harry, I must confess I was a little restive at first, for I was as hungry as an alligator; but I held the lamp to my feet, and thought of my Captain."

"What do you mean by your lamp and your Captain!" asked Harry.

"The Bible is the lamp I'm trying to use," said Jim. "You know we read, 'Thy word is a lamp unto my feet, and a light unto my path.' And what's the good of having a lamp, unless we use it to show us how to walk? When I felt like getting mad, I thought of the words, 'He that ruleth his spirit is better than he that taketh a city.' And then I said to myself, how would Jesus act if he were in my place? You know the Bible tells us that Jesus is 'the captain of our salvation.' I want to be a good soldier of Jesus. To do this, I must follow his example. So I prayed for grace to rule my own spirit, and follow the example of Jesus. This is what I mean, Harry," said Jim, "by holding the lamp to my feet, and thinking of my Captain."

Now Jim had the real spirit of a soldier. He was trying to follow the example of Jesus. And this is what we must do if we want to be "good soldiers of Jesus Christ."

I will only give you one other illustration of

the way in which we must follow the example of Jesus, and of the good we can do in this way.

This story is about a young man who was a sailor. He was an excellent sailor, and a good Christian man. He had first gone to sea as a sailor-boy, but had risen by degrees till he occupied the position of first mate, or chief officer on board a large ship that sailed from Boston. The young man's name was Palmer. Once when the vessel, in which Mr. Palmer sailed, came home to Boston, there was a change of captains. The old captain resigned, and a new one was appointed to command the ship. When a captain takes charge of a ship, he always likes to choose his own first mate, and generally he is allowed to do so. But in this case the owners of the ship insisted that Mr. Palmer should remain on board as the first mate. The captain was obliged to give way to them. This made him very angry, and he determined to do every thing he could to make Mr. Palmer's position on board the ship as uncomfortable as possible. And he certainly did this. He crossed him whenever he could. He found fault with every thing he did. He took every chance he could get of showing him disrespect before the crew, and tried to hurt his feelings in every possible way. But Palmer was a noble, Christian young man, and tried to follow the example of his Saviour. Yet he found it very hard.

Many a time, on the voyage, he said to himself: "There's no use talking about it; I can't stand this, and I won't." Then he would think: "Jesus, my master, would stand it, if he were in my place;" and this thought would lead him to overlook the captain's bad treatment, and try to do his duty in the best way he could.

The ship was on a trading voyage, which was to last for two years, and Palmer had shipped for the voyage. He felt that it would be a hard trial to go on, bearing all this so long. At every port they came to, he almost made up his mind to quit the ship. "But no," he said, "Jesus, when he was reviled, reviled not again; I will bear and forbear for his sake. I'll stand the voyage through." And so he did. Instead of paying "tit for tat," or answering crossly when he was crossly spoken to, he returned meekness and forgiveness for insult. He was always respectful to the surly old commander, and never neglected any of his duties. And so he kept on till the close of the voyage.

But at last the voyage ended. The ship came back to Boston. Then he made up his mind to quit at once. But, just as he was leaving the ship, the captain called him into his state-room, and stretching out his hand to him frankly said : —

"Mr. Palmer, I beg your pardon for all my bad conduct to you. I've treated you like a dog, and you have always behaved like a gentleman. I'm ashamed of myself, and so I ought to be. I was angry because I couldn't have my own mate; but you have been too much for me. I used to think that there was nothing in religion, but now I know there is. Your sort of spirit I've not been used to; it's beat me," — and tears came into the captain's eyes, — "it's fairly beat me. I've not heard many sermons, but you've preached me one two years long, and it's cured me of my mistake about religion. I used to think my old mate was a good one; but you are the best mate I ever had. I can't part with you, Mr. Palmer; I want you for the next voyage, and I'll try to make amends for my past bad conduct."

Mr. Palmer went with him. The captain treated him as kindly as though he had been his own son. At the end of that voyage, the captain left the ship, and recommended the owners to make Mr. Palmer captain. They did so, and a first-rate captain he made.

Now that honest sailor was a good soldier of Jesus Christ. He followed the example of Jesus, and we see how much good he did in that way.

Let us all try to be good soldiers of Jesus Christ. Remember the three things that we must do, if we want to be his soldiers.

We *must wear the uniform of Jesus.* We *must obey the orders of Jesus.* We *must follow the example of Jesus.* We cannot do any of these things in our own strength; but, if we

pray to Jesus for his grace, he will help us to
" fight manfully under his banner, and continue
his faithful soldiers and servants unto our life's
end."

VI.

THE CONQUEROR'S JEWEL.

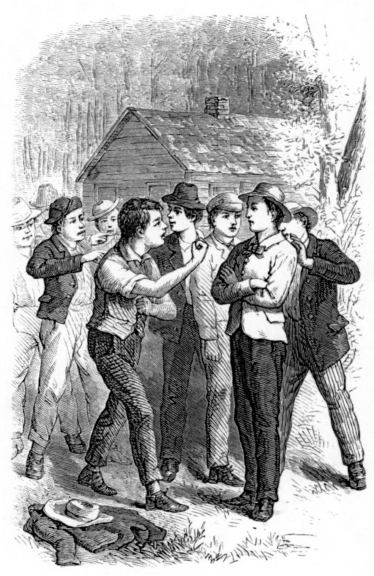

"The Conqueror's Jewel." — PAGE 178.

VI.

THE CONQUEROR'S JEWEL.

" An agate."—Exodus xxviii. 19.

This precious stone was regarded in old times as the conqueror's jewel. It was supposed, that if a person carried one of these jewels about with him, he would be sure to be successful in any thing that he undertook. In every conflict with evil, it would give him the victory. This conqueror's jewel we may consider as representing the grace of God. When we are called upon to fight against evil in any form, it is only the grace of God that can make us conquerors. The greatest enemy with which we have to fight is sin. This enemy meets us in many forms. But the form in which it gives us more trouble than any other is perhaps that of selfishness. This is an evil that is very hard to conquer.

Suppose we are walking in the country, and

meet a snake in the path; with the cane in our hand we strike it, again and again, till it lies still and motionless. We leave it, and go on our way, feeling sure that we have killed the snake. But when we have finished our walk, and come back to the place where we left the snake, we find it still alive and active. Then we say to ourselves, "Snakes are hard to kill." And it is just so with selfishness. It is a very difficult thing to conquer it. If we wish to subdue it, and get the victory over it, we must be sure to have this conqueror's jewel, the grace of God. And there are three things that this jewel will lead us to do in fighting against selfishness.

In the first place it will lead us — TO PRAY AGAINST IT.

Prayer is necessary to our success in every thing we do. Jesus said to his disciples: "Without me ye can do nothing." And this is as true now as it was then. It is as true of us as it was of the disciples. And it is particularly true of the thing we are now considering. If we want to get the victory over the selfishness of our own hearts, it is especially necessary for us to pray to Jesus to help us.

Here is an illustration in a story of two boys, who tried to get the victory over themselves in this way. These boys were brothers. One of them was named Henry and the other Martin. Henry was quick and passionate, while Martin was sullen and dogged in his disposition. They often quarrelled together, and sometimes about the merest trifles. Yet their mother was a good Christian woman, and tried to show them how wrong it was to give way to their bad tempers. And the boys really wanted to do better, but they did not seem to know how. Henry, the oldest, was at boarding-school. Christmas was coming, when he expected to go home to spend his vacation. He was very anxious to have a pleasant visit at home during the holidays; but he knew that if he and Martin got to quarrelling, as they generally did, it would spoil all their pleasure. So he wrote to his brother, some time before the close of the session, telling him that he hoped they should be able to get along more peaceably and pleasantly together, and suggesting a new plan for subduing their bad tempers and getting the victory over themselves.

Martin received Henry's letter very kindly, and agreed at once to adopt his plan; for he really wanted to be a good boy, and felt ashamed to think that two brothers could not live in their own home without quarrelling.

Well, the vacation time came. Henry arrived at home, and the holidays were passing away very pleasantly. Their mother was delighted to see how nicely the boys were getting on together. One day she told Henry how glad she was to see the great change which had taken place in himself and Martin.

"Yes, mother," said Henry, "we have felt a great deal happier, and have got on much more comfortably, since we have tried our new plan."

"Your new plan! What do you mean by that?" she asked with surprise.

"Why, you see, we have agreed to pray earnestly, every day, that God would help us not to give way to our bad tempers, and to get the victory over ourselves." — This was what Henry had written to Martin about before he came home at vacation. — "And then, besides praying," said Henry, "Martin has written down, on a piece of paper, a number of texts of scripture about temper. We each carry one of these pieces of paper in our pocket, and when I am tempted to be cross or he is tempted to be sulky, we take out our paper and read it, and in this way we feel that God is helping us very much. Here is my paper, mother;" and then Henry took it out, and read these verses : —

"Little children, love one another."

"Let not the sun go down upon your wrath."

"Leave off contention before it be meddled with."

"Be slow to speak, slow to wrath."

"Overcome evil with good."

"Bless them which persecute you : bless, and curse not."

"Let brotherly love continue."

"Be ye kind one to another, tender-hearted, forgiving one another."

Now, how interesting this was ! Henry and

Martin had each got this conqueror's jewel, the grace of God, and it was helping them to get the victory over their selfishness, by teaching them to pray. When the apostle Paul was on earth, he said: "I can do *all things* through Christ strengthening me." And you and I may say the same.

Edward Norton was a good, obedient boy. He was industrious in his studies, kind to his playfellows, and usually gentle in his manners; but he had one great fault, — a very quick, fiery temper. He would fly into a passion, in a moment, and when he was angry he did not seem to know, or care what he did. This made his mother very uneasy. She sometimes trembled, when she thought of what might happen some day, if her dear boy did not learn to control his temper, and get the victory over himself. She told him about the professor in a medical college in Boston, who got angry with a gentleman he was talking with, struck him a blow, and killed him on the spot. He was put in prison; tried; condemned; and hung as a murderer. And she used to say that, if that gentleman's mother had only taught him to control his temper, when a boy, he never would have become a murderer.

Edward was very fond of reading about the great generals, and conquerors of the world. His mother tried to teach him that the greatest, and best of all heroes, was the one who conquered himself. And, in order to fix this lesson on his mind, she made him repeat, every morning, for a week, the thirty-second verse of the sixteenth chapter of Proverbs, where Solomon says: "He that ruleth his spirit is better than he that taketh a city." And every day, as she did this, she taught him to pray that God would help him to control his temper, and give him the victory over himself.

On Saturday, at the close of this week, Edward was playing with some of his companions. Presently a difficulty arose. He said something about it, when one of the boys began to laugh at him. Edward grew very red in the face. His eyes were flashing with anger; he was doubling up his fist, and just going to strike the boy, when — suddenly he stopped. His hand was unclinched. His half-raised arm fell by his side. The boys did not know what it meant. But the thing that stopped him was the thought of Solomon's words, which he had been repeating all that week. As he remembered them, he offered a silent prayer, — " Lord help me." He tried to keep down his arm, and not speak the angry words. God heard his prayer, and helped him. He gained a splendid victory over himself. His fiery temper met with a Waterloo defeat that day. Edward could not play any more then. He made an excuse for leaving the boys. He ran home to his mother. As he entered the house he said : " I did it, mother ; I did it. God helped me, and I did it ; " and he burst into tears.

Here we see how Edward Norton had this conqueror's jewel, and how it gave him the victory over himself. The first thing that this conquering jewel, the grace of God, will do for us, in our fight against selfishness, is that *it will lead us to pray against it.*

The second thing that this conqueror's jewel will

lead us to do in getting the victory over selfishness is to — STRUGGLE AGAINST IT.

We must not think that praying is to take the place of striving. God only helps those who try to help themselves. Suppose that you and I have to climb up a high mountain. We kneel down at the foot of the mountain, and pray God to help us get up to the top of it. And then suppose we should sit down, and wait for God to send an angel, to take us in his arms, and carry us up to the top of the mountain. Have we any right to expect that God would help us in that way? Not at all. We might wait all our lives, but we never should get any help. If we want to get up the mountain, we must *begin* to climb, and we must *keep on* climbing till we get to the top, and *while we are doing this God will help us.* No soldier ever expects to gain the victory over his enemies without a hard struggle.

We have all read about the great victory which the Duke of Wellington obtained over the Emperor Napoleon at the battle of Waterloo. But he had to fight hard, all day, before he gained that victory. And so, if we want to get the victory over our selfishness, we must struggle hard against it.

Let me tell you about a boy named Archie Taylor, who struggled against his selfishness, and conquered it by giving way to his brother.

One day, after school, Archie came bounding into the house, crying: "Hurrah! hurrah! our school is going to have an excursion next Thursday. Hurrah! hurrah!"

"I'm glad of it, Archie," said his little sister, Amy, clapping her fat hands, and entering into her brother's joy.

"So am I," said Mrs. Taylor, his mother. "I am glad your teacher is so kind to his scholars. But *how* and *where* are you going, my dear?"

"We are going in two big wagons, mother, to River Point. We are to catch fish, and have a chowder and a clam-bake. Won't it be nice? Oh, I'm so glad! but where's the milk-pail? It's time to milk old Spotty."

Then he took the bright tin milk-pail, and went off, merry as a cricket, whistling Yankee Doodle.

"Oh, I'm so glad for Archie!" said little Amy to her mother, as soon as he was gone.

"Yes, it will be very pleasant for him," said Mrs. Taylor, "for what with milking Spotty, taking care of the pigs, doing up other chores, and going to school, he don't get much time for play. I'm very glad his teacher is going to give the school this treat."

Just then a stout boy, four years older than Archie, and covered with flakes, like snow, came into the cottage wearing a very bright look.

"Only think, mother," said he, "our fellows are going on an excursion next Thursday. Mr. Jones, our employer, has chartered a little steamboat to take all hands down the river to Bam's Island, where we are to have a glorious clambake. Isn't that jolly?"

"It is very kind indeed, in Mr. Jones," said Mrs. Taylor, "but I'm afraid you can't go, my son."

"Can't go!" exclaimed George, with great surprise; "pray, why not?"

"Be calm, George, and listen," said his mother. "Did you say the excursion was to be on Thursday?"

"Yes, ma'am, but what of that?"

"Well, Archie is going to River Point that day, and you know that both of you can't be from home the same day, because my arm is too lame to do the chores."

"Then let Archie stay at home: I won't," said George, in an angry tone.

"What's that you say?" asked Archie, who came in just then with his pail full of milk.

George told his story. Archie looked blank, and said: —

"I'm the youngest, and I told mother first. You ought to let me go, George."

"Well, I work hard in the mill all the time. You don't earn any money, and you ought to let *me* go," said George.

The boys would probably have got into a quarrel about it; but just then, their mother called them to tea, and told them not to say any thing more about it till the morning.

They sat round the table, and took their tea in silence that night, and with less pleasure than was usual in that humble cottage.

When supper was over, they had prayers

as usual. And when Mrs. Taylor came to pray for her children, she asked God to teach them to seek each other's happiness rather than their own; she prayed that he would help them to struggle against the selfishness of their own hearts, and to get the victory over it.

This prayer of their mother's set both the boys to thinking. It was hard for either to give up; yet, each felt it to be his duty to do so. Archie was the first to yield. It cost him a mighty struggle; but the next day, when George came home from work, he went to him, smiling in the greatest good humor and said : —

"George, you may go on Thursday, I'll stay at home."

"No, no, Archie," said George. "You may go, and I'll stay at home."

And now the two brothers had a very pleasant dispute about this. They both wanted to do right, and each, with great good-nature, pleaded to be allowed to stay at home. At last they agreed to leave it to their mother to decide which of them should go. She said :—

"George shall go because he works hard for us all the year. Archie will stay at home with me." This was certainly a wise decision. It settled the question at once.

On Thursday morning, George went down the river in the steamboat. Archie stayed with his mother and Amy. As he was getting a pail of water for his mother, his schoolmates rode by in the wagons. He felt pretty badly when he heard their merry shouts come ringing across the meadow. His heart was so full that he did not dare to stop and look after them. But, like an April cloud, this feeling of sadness soon passed away; and he felt happy again. His mother cooked a chicken for dinner; after that, she took Archie and Amy, and they had a walk along the brook, which ran past their cottage, and a nice long ramble through the woods. The day soon passed. George came home at the close of the day in excellent spirits; but, when they all went to bed at night, the happiest heart in that humble cottage was Archie's; for he had struggled against his selfishness, and had gotten the victory over it, by giving up his own pleasure for his brother's.

The next day, when the teacher found out the reason why Archie stayed at home, he was very much pleased. He spoke of it before the whole school, and praised him greatly. He said, Archie had set them a beautiful example, which he hoped they would all follow; that he had proved himself a real hero, and had gained a splendid victory over himself. Archie had this conqueror's jewel, — the true agate of the grace of God; and we see how it made him conqueror over selfishness.

The third thing, that this conqueror's jewel will lead us to do, in getting the victory over selfishness, is — TO REMEMBER THE EXAMPLE OF JESUS.

Jesus came down from heaven to do *three* things for us. The first was to fulfil God's law for us. The second was to die for our sins. The third was to show us how to live. The Bible tells us that " he left us an *example* that we should *follow his steps.*

You know, when we are learning to write, our teacher sets us a copy. Then we take the word or sentence, that has been written for us, letter by letter, and try to make others like them. And just in the same way, the life of Jesus is set before us as our copy. We are to keep it before us, and try to make our own lives like his. Being a Christian, means being like Jesus. Now it is said of Jesus that "*He pleased not himself.*" Would it not have been much pleasanter for him to have stayed in heaven, where all was holy and good; where everybody loved and honored him, and where the angels sang his praises, than to have come down to this dark, sinful world to live as a poor man, to suffer and to die upon the cross? Certainly. Would Jesus ever have consented to be our Saviour, if he had been trying to please himself? Never. He had the most perfect specimen of this conqueror's jewel that ever was; and it gave him a glorious victory. He was the most perfect conqueror of self. "He pleased not himself." Now, let me show how remembering the example of

Jesus helped a little girl to get the victory over her selfishness.

The name of this girl was Jeannette. She lived in Germany. One day, she went to see a grand review of troops in the town in which she lived. She found a very nice place where she could stand and see the soldiers as they marched by. She stood there and waited for them. Just after the soldiers began to march past that place, Jeannette saw a poor old woman behind her, trying very hard to get a peep at the soldiers. She pitied her very much, and said to herself : —

"I should like to see the soldiers march; but it isn't kind in me to stay in this nice seat, and let that old woman stand where she can't see any thing. Jesus pleased not himself. If I want to be like him I mustn't give way to selfishness. Then, too, I ought to honor old age, and I will."

So Jeannette called the old woman, and placing her in her nice seat, fell back herself among the crowd. There she had to stand on tiptoe, and dodge about, and peep, to catch a glimpse of the splendid procession that was marching by, when she might have seen it all easily if she had only kept her place. Some of the people near said she was a silly girl, and laughed at her. But she did not care for that. She felt that she had done right. And so she had. She was trying to be like Jesus. She remembered his example, and it helped her to get the victory over her selfishness; and this made her feel happier than if she had kept her seat, and seen all the soldiers marching. But this was not the end of it.

A few minutes after, a man, all covered with lace, elbowed his way through the crowd, and laying his hand on her shoulder, said: —

"Little girl, will you please come to her ladyship?"

Jeannette followed the man to the platform, inside of the crowd. A lady came up to her there and said: —

"My dear child, I saw you give your seat to that poor old woman. You did right. You acted nobly. God will bless you, my child, for what you have done. I hope you will always try and act in this way. Now sit down here by me, where you can see every thing."

This little girl had the conqueror's jewel, — the Bible agate, — and it helped her to get the victory over her selfishness by *remembering the example of Jesus.*

I have only one more story to tell you, and that is about a boy who had this jewel, and was helped by it in the same way. His name was Roger Seymour.

He came home from school one day, and, flinging down his hat, he said: "It's no use trying any longer, mother: I must give up and go to fighting, as all the other boys do."

His mother looked sadly at him for a moment, and said: "My dear boy, try a little longer for my sake."

"Mother, I've tried, and tried, until the boys all hoot at me, and call me a coward. I don't care so much for that, either: but they say, even the best boys in the school, that they can't respect a boy who won't fight; and I'm sure I don't want to lose the respect of my schoolmates. Mother, you don't know the boys in this town : it seems really necessary to fight now and then, or they'll think you have no spirit."

" I can't bear to think of my son engaging in a street fight, even to gain the respect of his companions," said his mother.

" And I can't bear to think that none of the boys respect me," said Roger, as he went out of the room.

Mrs. Seymour felt very sorry that Roger should have so much trouble in school. But yet she could never think of advising him to put himself on a level with the brutes, by fighting, like a bull-dog, or a bear. She knew that Roger was right in refusing to fight. She felt sure that, if he only kept on in this way, by and by the very boys, who were now the most forward in urging him to fight, would come to have the greatest respect for him, for this very reason, — that he would not fight. So she resolved to try and encourage him all she could, by talking to him about Jesus, and getting him to try and keep his blessed example before him all the time.

Before Roger went to bed that night, she had

a nice long talk with him. She told him how Jesus was treated when on earth, — she reminded him of the names he was called, — a glutton, a wine-drinker, a Samaritan (that was considered the name of greatest reproach then), and even a devil! And yet, *He* never fought. He never struck any one a blow. He never spoke a cross, or angry word to anybody. "When he was reviled, he reviled not again." "Like a lamb before her shearers, he opened not his mouth."

"Remember, Roger," said she, "that Jesus was once a boy, and he knows just how boys feel. As he was the best man that ever lived, so he was the best boy. And the boys who lived in Palestine, when Jesus was on earth, were quite as bad as the boys who live here now. No doubt they did every thing they could to provoke Jesus, and make him angry. But he never quarrelled with them. He never fought one of them. His example is the best, and the noblest for us to imitate. And we must try to be like him, if we wish to be good, and great, and happy."

12

"O mother!" said Roger, "when you talk to me, I feel sure that you are right, and it seems as if it would be easy for me to do as you wish; but, when I am with the boys, they talk so differently that they make me think you are too particular. How shall I keep from being influenced by them, mother?"

"You must pray; you must strive; and you must think of Jesus. This is the only way to get the victory in such cases," said his mother.

After this, Roger felt more resolved than ever to keep on in the right way.

And it was very well he did feel so; for, just after that, the boys renewed their attacks upon him with more force than ever. They seemed determined to make him fight. But he was equally determined that he would not do it.

One day, just before school, they had been trying very hard to get up a quarrel with him. But he refused.

"Coward! coward!" was the cry all round; "he's afraid to fight!"

"Afraid? yes, I *am* afraid to do what *I know*

is wrong; and you can't make me do it," said Roger, calmly, as he turned from them and went into school.

Oh, what hard work this was ! for though he knew it was right, it made him sad to feel that the boys all thought him a mean and cowardly fellow. And this is just one of the hardest things we have to bear in this life.

He had been carrying on this great battle with none but God on his side, for all the boys were arrayed against him; but, remember, one with God on his side is in the majority. His teacher had been watching carefully the trial that he was passing through. He was delighted to see the stand that Roger had taken. He admired the true courage, the real heroism which he showed. He was glad that he had one brave boy in his school who had manliness and courage enough about him to refuse to fight. And now, he thought it was time for him to step in to Roger's help. This teacher was accustomed to talk very freely to the boys about any thing that happened. So the first time that

Roger was absent from school, he took occasion to say to them: —

"Boys, do any of you know Roger Seymour?"

"Yes, sir, I do," said one.

"So do I," said another.

"And so do I," said a third.

"We *all* know Roger, sir," said a fourth boy.

"Do you?" asked the teacher. "I thought you would say that, and yet I don't think that any of you really know him at all; for I have often heard you call him a coward, and say that he wouldn't fight; when, the fact is, if *you* knew him as well as I do, you would know that he was fighting every day, and that he really did more fighting than any of you."

"Why, we never saw him fighting," said several of the boys. "Pray, sir, who does he fight with?"

"With *himself*."

"Fight with himself! how can he do that?" asked the boys.

"In this way," said the teacher. "You have often provoked him: he forgave you, because he

is trying to follow the example of the meek and
gentle Jesus.   Then you taunted him, and
called him ' coward.'   He knew that he was not
a coward, and he longed to show you that he
was not one.   He felt that, by one blow of his
strong right arm, he could have put a stop to
your persecution of him : but he would not
displease his mother; he would not do what
she had taught him was wrong.   And so he has
gone on, day after day, struggling against his
own feelings.   The battle has been a hard one,
but he has come off conqueror.   I feel proud of
such a scholar.   I tell you, boys, Roger Seymour is a real hero.   He is the bravest boy
in the school, for *he has conquered himself.*
And the Bible says : 'He that ruleth his own
spirit is better than he that taketh a city.' "

After that day, Roger had no more trouble in
school.   No one called him a coward again ;
but they all respected and honored him more
than any boy in school.

Now Roger Seymour had this conqueror's
jewel,— the true agate,— the grace of God, and
you see how it made him conqueror. Selfishness

was the enemy over which this jewel gave him the victory. And we have spoken of three things that this conqueror's jewel, the grace of God, will help us to do in fighting against selfishness. The first is, *to pray against* it; the second is, *to struggle against* it; and the third is *to remember the example of Jesus.*

I hope, my dear young friends, you will all try to get this precious jewel. You never can fight against the sin of selfishness unless you have it. And you must either fight against it and conquer it, or give yourselves up to it and be its slaves. Now to be the slave of selfishness is a terrible thing. Jesus came into the world, as the Captain of our salvation, on purpose to save us from this sad state. Oh! pray earnestly to him to give you his grace, and to put this conqueror's jewel round your neck; then you will be able to struggle against selfishness and conquer it. This is the most splendid and important of all victories. May God help you all to gain it for Jesus' sake. Amen.

VII.

THE WONDERFUL EYES.

VII.

THE WONDERFUL EYES.

" The eyes of the Lord are in every place." — PROVERBS xv. 3.

WHEN we are very much pressed with engagements, it would sometimes be a great convenience if we could manage to be in two places at the same time. But we know that this is impossible. However much we may try, *this* is something that we cannot do. And it is not only true that *we* cannot do it; but it is equally true that the best, and wisest, and greatest persons in the world cannot do it.

Suppose that a convention should be held in the great city of London next year, to consider this subject, and this convention was to be composed of five hundred of the best and wisest men that have lived from the beginning of the world. Suppose that Abraham, and Moses, and Job, and Solomon, and Elijah, and Isaiah, and Daniel, and Peter, and John, and Paul, were to be members of that convention; and Christopher Columbus, and Martin Luther, and George Washington, and Benjamin Franklin, and Sir Isaac Newton, and Sir Humphry Davy, and others of the same character, were to be there; what a wonderful convention that would be!

How interesting it would be to see those great and good men, and hear them talk! And suppose that with all the wisdom and knowledge they had when they were in this world, and with all the higher wisdom gained since they left this world, they should spend a week or a month in trying to find out some way in which a person might be in New York, or Boston, or London, at the same time; they never would succeed. However much a man may know, and however wise and good and great he may be, still he can only be present in one place at a time. This is as true of angels as it is of men. The angels can go very quickly from one place to another; but still, even the angels can only be in one place at a time. We may learn to travel much faster than we can do now. How much faster a locomotive travels than a snail! Now, it is possible that we may learn, by and by, to travel as much quicker than the fastest locomotive goes now, as that exceeds the snail's slowness. Perhaps we may learn to go as fast as a cannon-ball goes when shot from a gun. We may even learn to go as fast as light travels. This is two hundred thousand miles in a second. Only think of this! At that rate, we could go to California, and back again, more than ten times in a single tick of a watch, or snap of a finger. But even if we could travel at that rate, we could only be in one place at a time. But the Bible tells us that what is impossible with men is possible with God. He can be, not in *two* places only at the same time; but in twenty, or in five hundred. Nay, "the eyes of the Lord are in *every* place."

But suppose some one should say this only means that God keeps moving about from one place, without being in every place at the same time, how can we prove that this is not so, but that he really is in every place at the same time? There is one short and easy way of

proving this.   Here it is : God knows all that
everybody thinks, and feels, and says, and does ;
and, therefore, he must be always present with
everybody.   *This* is one of the most wonderful
things about God.   And it is one of the things
in which there is the greatest difference between
ourselves and God.   We can only be in *one*
place at a time; but, " the eyes of the Lord are
in every place."

Our present purpose is to speak about " The
Wonderful Eyes."   There are three things that
these eyes are intended to do, and on account
of which they may well be called wonderful.

*The first thing for which " the eyes of the Lord
are in every place" is for* — WARNING.

You know when there are dangerous rocks at
the entrance of a harbor, it is usual to build
a light-house near them.   The light-house is put
there, on purpose, to give warning to the sailors
of the danger to which they are exposed from
those rocks.

There is safety in the light thus given.   It
used to be the custom with store-keepers, to
have strong window-shutters to their store-

windows. When night came, they would close those shutters, and fasten them very tight with iron bolts or bars. This was done to keep the robbers out. But now, it is getting to be the custom, not to have shutters at all to the stores. The windows are left, with perhaps only a grating of wire before them. But the gas is kept lighted in the store. If robbers should get into the store at night, the watchman, or any one else going by, could see them in a moment. The light in those stores is a better protection than the strongest shutters that could be made. Do you suppose that any person would be willing to go into a store and steal, if he knew that some one was looking at him all the time? No. And so if people would only remember that "the eyes of the Lord are in every place," it would be like leaving the window open, and the gas burning. It would be a warning against sin. Joseph remembered this; and, when he was tempted to do something very wrong, he said: "How can I do this great wickedness, and sin against God?" The thought of God's eye being upon him was a warning to him. And so it will be to us. Do you think men would ever allow themselves to lie, or swear, or steal, or commit murder, if they could hear the voice of God speaking to them, or see the eye of God looking at them all the time? No. This is what David meant when he said, "I have set the Lord always before me: he is at my right hand, therefore shall I not fall." To *fall* here means to sin, or to do any thing wrong. He felt that, so long as he remembered that God was near him, and looking at him, it would be a warning or safeguard, to keep him from committing sin. It is only because we forget what the Bible tells us about God seeing us; or because we do not believe it, that we fall into sin.

Let me tell you of a dreadful case of wickedness, which might have been prevented, if the words of the text had only been remembered.

There were three girls in the same class in a boarding-school. Their names were Jane, and Lucy, and Mary. Jane was the best scholar of the three. She kept at the head of her class all the time. Lucy was not as smart as Jane;

but she was very amiable and loving, and she and Jane were bosom friends. Mary was neither as bright a girl as Jane, nor as good a girl as Lucy. She was ill-tempered and jealous. It used to make her angry that she could neither recite her lessons as well as Jane, nor be as much of a favorite as Lucy was. She envied Jane her success, in keeping at the head of her class, and Lucy her amiability, which made everybody love her so. She let this wicked feeling stay in her heart. It grew worse and worse. From envy it turned to hatred. This feeling grew stronger and stronger in her bosom, till it seemed to take entire possession of it. At last she made up her mind to have revenge on her classmates in a most awfully wicked way.

At different times, she got small quantities of poison, till she thought she had enough to kill one, or both, of her classmates; then she waited for an opportunity to give it to them.

This came rather sooner than she expected. Jane, the one whom she hated most, was taken sick with a cold. Her friend Lucy waited on her, and nursed her like a sister. One evening, Mary was in the room with them. Lucy was preparing a cooling drink of lemonade for her sick friend. While she was busy in another part of the room, Mary contrived, without being seen, to slip the poison into the tumbler. Soon after, without knowing what had taken place, the kind-hearted girl, Lucy, took up the tumbler, and carried it to Jane to drink. But, happily for her, she had just fallen into a sound sleep. In the mean time Mary had left the room. She supposed, of course, that the lemonade had been taken; but it was left on the table untasted. Soon after, a servant came in; and, as Jane was still asleep, the tumbler of lemonade was carried out with some other things, and left on the table in the dining-room. Supposing that the poisoned drink was doing its deadly work, this wicked girl, in going up to her own room passed through the dining-room. Seeing a glass of lemonade on the table, and feeling thirsty, she picked it up and drank it. How awful the punishment which overtook her! *It was the same tumbler which she had intended should be the means of killing one of her classmates, whom she hated most, and of fixing the blame of the dreadful deed on the other.* The deadly draught which she had designed for another, God in his mysterious providence had caused her to drink herself!

She was soon taken with terrible sickness. Her awful screams rang through the house. The family gathered round her bed, and were filled with horror when they heard, from the wicked girl's own lips, the dreadful deed she had done; and how God had caused her to fall into the very snare which she had laid for another. She died in fearful agony.

Now, suppose that, when the thought of this horrible wickedness first came into the mind of this unhappy girl, she had remembered the words of our text, — " The eyes of the Lord are in every place;" suppose she had felt that God was looking right into her heart, and that he was angry with her for her wickedness, — do you think she would have gone on to do what she did? No. The thought of those wonderful eyes would have been a warning to her. It would have kept her from committing that great sin.

Some hundreds of years ago, in what are called " the Middle Ages," the great lords and knights of the world were always at war with each other. In those days there was a celebrated duke, who lived in a great castle. One of this man's neighbors had offended him, and he resolved to take vengeance on him. It happened, soon after he had made up his mind to do this, that he heard his enemy was about to pass near his castle with only a few men with him. It was a good opportunity to take his revenge, and he was determined not to let it pass.

He had a minister of the gospel living in the castle, who was his chaplain. He told him what he was going to do. The chaplain tried to persuade him to give it up, but in vain. He said a great deal to the duke about the sin of what he was about to do, but still he was resolved to go on. Finding that all his arguments had no effect on the duke, the chaplain said to him : —

" Well, my Lord, since I cannot persuade you
to give up this plan of yours, will you, at least,
come into the chapel that we may pray together
before you go."

The duke consented, and the chaplain and he
knelt down together in prayer. Then the
minister said to him : " Will you please repeat
after me, sentence by sentence, the prayer which
our blessed Saviour taught his disciples."

" I will," said the duke.

And so they began, and went on. The chaplain said a sentence, and the duke repeated it,
till they came to the petition : " Forgive us our
trespasses, as we forgive those who trespass
against us." Here the duke stopped.

" My Lord, you are silent," said the chaplain. " Please go on, and repeat the words
after me, ' Forgive us our trespasses, as we forgive those who trespass against us.' "

" I can't do it," said the duke.

" Well, then, God cannot forgive you for he
has said so. He himself has given us this
prayer. Therefore, you must either give up
your revenge, or give up saying this prayer :

for to ask God to pardon you as you are pardoning your enemy, is to ask him to take vengeance on you for all your sins. Go now, my Lord, and meet your enemy. In the same way God will meet you at the last day."

This was more than the duke could stand. His stubborn will gave way under it.

"No," said he, " I will finish my prayer : My God, my Father, pardon me ; forgive me, as I desire to forgive him who has offended me ; lead me not into temptation, but deliver me from evil ! "

" Amen," said the chaplain.

" Amen," repeated the duke, who now understood the Lord's prayer better than he had ever done before, because he had begun to practise it.

Now, the only way to make men feel that God is present with them, and looking at them, is by causing them to understand his word. God can see us in other ways, but we can only see him, clearly and properly, through the truths of the Bible. And so, you see that, when that chaplain was trying to make the duke understand the meaning of that part of the Lord's prayer, he was really trying to bring him to a point where he would see, and feel that the eyes of God were on him; that he was watching all the feelings of his heart, and was writing them down in his book, to judge him for them at last. And as soon as he saw that "the eyes of the Lord" were upon him, in this way, it was a solemn warning to him which he could not neglect. It made him give up at once his sinful feelings of revenge. If that wicked school girl could have been made to feel that God's eyes were on her, it would have kept her from the great sin she committed, and have saved her life. And so we see how the revengeful duke was led to give up his sin as soon as he felt that God's eyes were on him. "The eyes of the Lord are in every place." The first thing for which they are there is for *warning.*

The second thing for which these wonderful eyes are present is for — ENCOURAGEMENT.

When Moses was leading the children of Israel, through the wilderness, from Egypt to the land of Canaan, he had a great many heavy trials to bear, and a great many hard duties to perform. He needed a great deal of encouragement in bearing those trials, and doing those duties. And the way in which he got that encouragement was, by remembering that God was with him, and his wonderful eyes were watching him all the time. This is what St. Paul means, when, in speaking about the trials of Moses in the wilderness, he said that "he endured as *seeing him who is invisible.*" He remembered that these wonderful eyes, which are in every place, were with him even there. He went about all the time, feeling, and saying to himself, — "Thou God seest me." And this gave *him* encouragement, and it will do the same to us. If we learn to see " Him who is invisible," that is if we always remember that " the eyes of the Lord " are upon us, night and day, wherever we go, it will give us encouragement both to *suffer*, and to *do* what God appoints for us.

There is a story told of the MacGregors, a Highland clan in Scotland, which illustrates this part of our sermon very well. There was a severe battle fought between the English and the Scotch, at a place called Prestonpans, in the year 1745. In the course of this battle the chieftain of the MacGregor clan was struck by two balls, at the same moment, and fell to the ground. This disheartened his soldiers very much. They thought their beloved chieftain was dead, and having no one to lead them, their ranks began to waver, and they were just on the point of turning their backs on the enemy, and retreating from the field of battle, when their wounded chief raised himself up on his elbow, and, as the blood streamed from his wounds, cried out : —

" I am not dead, my children : I am looking at you. Do your duty like brave men." Those few words had a wonderful effect on the men. All thought of retreating was given up. They were inspired with fresh courage. They felt that the eyes of their chief were upon them, and they plunged into the thickest of the fight, resolved to do honor to the name they bore.

And if we remember that, wherever we go, " the eyes of the Lord " are upon us, and he is watching us all the time, it will be a great encouragement to us. If we have trials to bear, there is nothing that will encourage us like the thought that God's wonderful eyes are watching us.

A gentleman was talking with a poor woman in his neighborhood, whose case was very trying. She had not been very long married before her husband was taken very ill. He got better after a while, but the disease had fastened itself upon him. He was liable to be attacked by it every few days. This made him unfit to do much work, and even when he did work a little he suffered dreadfully. This was a great trial. Here was a young woman just starting in her married life, when a dark cloud seemed to settle down on her. She was disappointed in all the comfort and happiness she had looked forward to when she was married. Now, she had nothing to expect but sickness, and suffering to her husband, and a long struggle with poverty and want for herself and family. She was a Christian woman, as her answer showed when the gentleman asked her if she did not feel very unhappy, as she thought of the trial that was before her. "Well, sir," she said, "I dare say I should; but when I saw the trouble coming I made up my mind never to forget these two things; God sees it all, and he knows what is best. And *when I think that his eyes are upon me, I feel encouraged to bear up.*"

Yes, "the eyes of the Lord are in every place" on purpose to encourage his people.

The third thing for which these wonderful eyes "*are in every place*" *is* — TO HELP.

A lady, in one of our large cities, had been in the habit of attending the evening meetings of the church to which she belonged. Sometimes she had no one to go with her, and then she never hesitated to go alone, rather than stay away. Some of her friends used to tell her that it was a dangerous thing, and they tried to persuade her that she had better give it up; but she always said that the Lord was present in the street, as well as in the church, and she felt sure that he would take care of her. One evening, in coming home from church, as she was crossing a public walk that lay in her way, and where it was quite lonely, two ruffians stopped her, and, holding a pistol to her breast, demanded her watch and her money. But although alone, as they supposed, there was one with her in whom she trusted, though they could not see him. It was that same Saviour at whose presence, when he was on earth, a whole band of men once "went backward and fell to the earth." As there was no one but Jesus to protect her, this Christian lady instantly fell on her knees before the robbers, and with uplifted hands, cried out: "Now, Lord Jesus, help me!" This was something for which the robbers were not prepared. They were frightened, and ran away, leaving her, all untouched, to go home in peace, rejoicing in that God whose "eyes are in every place," and who is a very present help in time of trouble.

One of the principal ways in which God helps his people to do right, is by causing them to understand his word, and feel its power; and when some verse of Scripture is explained to us, and set before us in such a way as to make a deep impression on our minds, then it is just as if God's wonderful eyes were fixed upon us, to lead us to do something which he wants to have done, and to help us to do it. Let me give you an illustration of this.

Julia Morrison was a Sunday-school girl, about thirteen or fourteen years old. She was a Christian girl, and took the greatest delight in her Sunday school, because she loved the Bible so much, and found such great pleasure in studying it there. One day their lesson in school had been on that passage of Scripture in which these words are found : "Whatsoever thy hand findeth to do, do it with thy might; for there is no work, nor device, nor knowledge, nor wisdom, in the grave, whither thou goest." The teacher said a great deal about the importance of doing *at once* whatever we have to do. She said, when any duty was before us which we ought to do, we should feel as if the eyes of the Lord were upon us, and he was watching to see if we did it. The teacher's words made a deep impression on Julia's mind. She kept thinking about them all the way home. She said to herself: "I'll always try to remember the lesson of to-day. I'll think I see God's eyes looking straight at me, when I have any thing to do, and I'm sure it will keep me from putting off things. It will help me to do what ought to be done right away ; and it will help me to do it well too, or, as the Bible says, ' with my might.'"

When Julia reached home, she found her father sitting in an easy-chair by the fire, doing nothing. Mr. Morrison was a member of the church, but he was not a very active Christian. He had undertaken to be a tract distributor in a district of the town, not far from where he lived. He generally took a Sunday afternoon, once a month, to distribute his tracts ; but he did not like the work much, and was glad of any excuse for putting it off. It so happened that *that* afternoon was the time for doing this good work. But it had rained a little, and was rather damp, so he had concluded not to go on that day.

When Julia came in, she saw the bundle of tracts lying on the table, and said : —

"Why, pa, haven't you been round with your tracts to-day?"

"No, my dear?"

"Aren't you going with them, pa?"

"Not to-day, my dear. It's too damp."

Then Julia's lesson came into her mind, and she thought this was a good opportunity to begin to practise it. She had often been with her father when he distributed the tracts. She knew all the places where they were left, and she liked to do it very much, for she felt it was doing something for Jesus. It seemed to her that it was *her* work as much as her father's. When she saw the bundle of tracts on the table, she felt as if the eyes of the Lord were upon her, watching to see what she would do. That thought helped her very much. So she said:—

"O, pa, let me go with you. I've got my bonnet on, and it won't take me long."

"No, no! It's too damp for you to go out again. It'll do as well some other day."

"See, it's not raining now, pa. I'll take the big umbrella, in case it should rain again. The

people will want the tracts.   Do, please, let me
go, pa."

Seeing how earnest she was about it, he said
she might go.   So Julia took the tracts, and
started.   She knew the district well, and felt
very happy to think that she was working for
Jesus.   In the course of her walk she came
to a large, old house, with a big knocker on
the door.   She rapped again and again, but
no one answered.   The poor girl's patience was
almost worn out, when she thought she heard a
sound in the house.   She gave another knock,
and the door was opened by a middle-aged
woman who wore a good dress, but whose face,
Julia thought, looked very unhappy.

With a sweet, pleasant smile she handed her
a tract, and then went on her way till her work
was done.   When her tracts were all given
away, she went home; but, in doing so, how
little she thought that, by her walk that damp
afternoon, she had been the means of saving a
soul from death and a body from the grave.

And yet, it was even so.   For it was afterwards found out that the woman at whose door

Julia had waited so long, was in a great deal of trouble. She had got to be so gloomy, and unhappy, that she did not want to live any longer. She had made up her mind to hang herself, and was in the very act of doing this, when this dear girl gave the first knock at her door. The rope was fastened to the high post of an old-fashioned bedstead; the noose, or slip-knot, was round her neck, and she was going to jump off the bedstead, and rush into the presence of God, when that knock came at the door. This startled her. She waited a moment. There was another knock. She waited longer. Again and again the knock came. She felt vexed and angry; but she concluded to go and see what it was all about. She took the rope off from her neck, and went to the door to see who had disturbed her. She opened the door. The sweet, loving, happy look, which that dear child gave her, took away all her angry feelings in a moment. She received the tract, and concluded to sit down and read it through, before going upstairs again to carry out her wicked purpose. She did so. God blessed the reading of that tract to her soul's good. It showed her what a sinner she was. It led her to Jesus. She became a Christian, and then she went to Julia's father, and told him what a blessing his daughter's visit to her house had been.

Here you see, that it was the thought of God's wonderful eyes being upon her, which helped this dear child to "do with her might what her hand found to do" that afternoon, and how much good came from what she did.

"The eyes of the Lord are in every place." These eyes are wonderful for three things. They are wonderful *to warn;* wonderful *to encourage;* and wonderful *to help.*

My dear young friends, if you will only take the words of this text, and keep them before you all the time; if you will only think about these wonderful eyes, and remember that you never, for one moment, can get away from them, — it will be a blessing to you all your days. It will be a warning, — an encouragement, — a help.

I will finish this subject with some simple lines which would do us all good if we would learn them and remember them. They were written on the words of our text; " The eyes of the Lord are in every place : —

" God can see me every day,
When I work, and when I play ;
When I read and when I talk,
When I run and when I walk ;
When I eat and when I drink,
When I sit and only think ;
When I laugh and when I cry, —
God is ever watching nigh.

When I'm quiet, when I'm rude,
When I'm naughty, when I'm good ;
When I'm happy, when I'm sad,
When I'm sorry, when I'm glad ;
When I pluck the fragrant rose,
That in my neat garden grows ;
When I crush the tiny fly, —
God is watching from the sky.

When the sun gives heat and light,
When the stars are twinkling bright ;
When the moon shines on my bed, —
God still watches o'er my head ;
Kindly guiding lest I stray,
Pointing to the happy way,
Night or day, at church or fair,
God is near me everywhere."

14

VIII.

ACKNOWLEDGING GOD.

"Acknowledging God." — PAGE 230.

VIII.

ACKNOWLEDGING GOD.

" In all thy ways acknowledge him."—PROVERBS iii. 6.

AMONG the studies that we have to attend to when going to school are spelling and definitions.

We all know something about these studies. We have had many a lesson of this kind. Well, suppose we try our hand at it again. We may begin our sermon to-day with an exercise in the old line of spelling and definition. There is a word of three syllables which we may spell and define, as a sort of introduction to our sermon. The word to which I refer is not a hard one. It is the word — *atheist.*

If I should ask one of you to spell it for me, you would stand up and say — a-t h e — athe — i s t, atheist.

And then, suppose I should turn to some one who was further advanced, to some one who has a little college learning, and understands about Latin and Greek, and ask him for a *definition* of the word atheist. He would tell me, in a minute, that this word is made up of two Greek words; viz., the Greek letter alpha, or a, which means no; and the Greek word theos, which means God. So that the real definition of this word is — no God. And if you want to know what kind of a person an *atheist* is, according to the definition of this word he is a *no-god-man*. He is a man who *has* no God; who says or thinks there is no God.

The Bible tells us that such a man is a fool. The Psalmist says, "The *fool* hath said in his heart — no God."

Sir Isaac Newton was one of the most learned men that ever lived. He was an astronomer; that is, he studied all about the stars and other heavenly bodies. He was also a good Christian man. But there was another learned man, and astronomer, who used to visit him sometimes, whose name was Halley. This man was an atheist, a no-god-man. He told Sir Isaac, one day, that he did not believe any one ever made the great worlds which they studied about. He thought they just happened to come where they were.

Sir Isaac wanted to show him the folly of thinking so. In order to do this, he had two globes made,—one to represent the earth, and the other to represent the sky. They were finished in the most beautiful manner. When they were done, he had them placed on the table in the midst of his study, and then invited his friend Halley to come and see him. As soon as he entered the study, his eye rested on the globes. He hastened up to them, and asked, in admiration : " Why, Newton, who made these ? "

" Nobody made them," said Sir Isaac.

" Pooh ! pooh ! " cried Halley ; " then how in the world did they get here ? "

" They just happened here," said he.

" O, nonsense, man, somebody must have made them, for how could they get here of themselves ? "

Then Sir Isaac began and reasoned seriously with him about his own folly, in refusing to believe that those poor little globes could exist without a maker, or come there of themselves, while the great globe on which he lived, and the other worlds around it, he thought had no Maker, but just came by chance.

There are very few people in the world who are willing to profess themselves atheists, or to deny with their *lips* that there is a God; but there are a great many people who deny God in their lives. They live as if there were no God. They are *practical* atheists. Solomon's words, in the text, are intended to keep us from being like them. Our text says to each of us: " In all thy ways acknowledge him;" that is, God. To acknowledge God, means to own or to confess him. It means that we should admit that there is a God, and then try to live and act, all the time, as if we *believed* what we said.

But what is there about God that we should acknowledge ? This is the question for us to answer. And in trying to answer this question, I wish to show that there are *three* things connected with God which we should acknowledge.

The first thing about God we should acknowledge is — his PRESENCE.

The Bible teaches us that "the eyes of the Lord are in *every place,* beholding the evil and the good." In the one hundred and thirty-ninth Psalm, David asks the solemn question: "Whither shall I go from thy spirit, or whither shall I flee from thy presence? If I ascend up into heaven, thou art there: if I make my bed in hell, thou art there. If I take the wings of the morning, and dwell in the uttermost parts of the sea; even there shall thy hand lead me, and thy right hand shall hold me. If I say, Surely the darkness shall cover me; even the night shall be light about me. Yea, the darkness hideth not from thee; but the night shineth as the day: the darkness and the light are both alike to thee." How beautifully Dr. Watts has expressed this thought in one of his sweet hymns, when he says: —

> " Among the deepest shades of night
>   Can there be one who sees my way ?
> Yes, God is as a shining light
>   That turns the darkness into day.
>
> When every eye around me sleeps
>   May I not sin without control ?

No ; for a constant watch he keeps
    On every thought, of every soul.

If I could find some cave, unknown,
    Where human feet had never trod,
Yet *there*, I could not be alone,
    On every side there would be God."

All people except an atheist, a no-god-man, will admit the truth of this with their lips, and yet very few admit it in their lives. Yes, very few people indeed live, all the time, as if they believed God was present with them, watching what they did, listening to what they said, and reading all their thoughts and feelings, and writing every thing down in his great book of remembrance. If we only did this, it would soon make good Christians of us all. In reading the Bible, you will notice, that all the good people of God whose histories are written there, acknowledged God's presence. They seemed to act, and speak, and live, all the time, as if they felt that God was looking at them. Look at Joseph in the house of Potiphar, in Egypt. He is tempted to do what would have been very wrong. And how does he overcome the temptation ? By acknowledging God's presence. He says — "How *can* I do this great wickedness, and *sin against God?*" He felt that God was looking at him all the time, and this kept him from committing sin.

Look at Moses. You remember what great trials, and troubles, he had to pass through, in getting the whole nation of the Israelites out from Egypt, and then leading them, for forty years, up and down that waste howling wilderness. Why, when we think of all the immense labors he had to perform, and the heavy burdens, and cares, that pressed upon him continually, we cannot help wondering how he ever could endure them all. But the Bible explains it very satisfactorily. It tells us that, "he endured *as seeing him who is invisible.*" This means that he acknowledged God's presence. He felt that God was with him continually. He seemed to see God looking at him, wherever he went, and whatever he was doing. This made his duties easy, and his burdens light.

It was just the same with the other good men

of whom we read in the Bible. And if we want
to be like them, we must acknowledge God's
presence as they did.   We must try to get this
great thought fixed on our minds — " *Thou God
seest me.*"   Do you think you would ever tell a
lie, if you remembered that God's ear was close
to your lips when you were speaking it, and
that he would write it down at once in his
book ! No, certainly not.   Or do you think
you would ever allow yourself to do any thing
you knew was wrong, if you could see the eye
of God looking directly at you, while you were
doing it ?   Of course not.   It is only when
we forget God's presence, and become prac_
tical atheists, that we can go on and commit
sin.

A mother once told her little boy to go to a
carpenter's shop and get some chips. " But,"
said the boy, " the carpenter isn't there now,
and if he was there, he wouldn't let me have
them."   " Never mind that," said his mother,
" you can go and take them, and he won't know
any thing about it."   " But," said the little boy,
" God will know it, though."   This good boy

acknowledged God's presence; but his mother acted like an atheist, like a no-god-woman.

There was a very learned man once, whose name was Linnæus. He was a great botanist, and wrote a great deal about plants and flowers. He was a pious man, and had a constant sense of God's presence. In order to assist him in remembering that God's eye was always on him, he had these words written over his study door, — "*Live innocently, God is present.*"

There was a man once, who was in the habit of going to his neighbor's corn-field to steal grain. One day he took his son with him, a little fellow about eight years of age. When they reached the place, the father told him to hold the bag, while he looked round to see if anybody was watching. He peeped through all the rows of corn, and got upon the fence, and looked all round without seeing any one. Then he took the bag from the child, and began to fill it. "O father!" said the boy, "you have forgotten to look one way." He dropped the bag in a fright, and said : "Which way, child ?"— supposing some one saw him. "You forgot to look up to the sky, to see if God was watching," said the little boy. The father felt this rebuke of his child so much, that he left the corn in the field, returned to his home, and never ventured to steal again.

There was a little girl whose name was Anna. Her parents were not Christians. They never prayed. When they gathered round the table to their meals, they never asked a blessing, or acknowledged God as the giver of all their mercies. And when the day was passed, they lay down at night, I will not say like heathen, but like animals, never thanking God for all his favors, or asking him to take care of them while they slept.

At length, there came a pious uncle to spend a few weeks with them. During his stay, he was invited to ask a blessing on their meals, and to conduct family worship.

The morning after he had left them, the family gathered round the table, and were about to commence their breakfast without a word of blessing, when little Anna who sat next her father looked up to him, and whispered: " Is

ACKNOWLEDGING GOD.   223

there no God to-day, papa?" This touching
question of his child went straight to his heart.
It led him to think about his forgetfulness of
God, and he soon became a Christian.

A lady was once in a dreadful storm at sea.
In speaking of it, she says: "We were for many
hours tossed about in sight of dangerous rocks.
The steam-engines would work no longer; the
wind raged violently, and all around were heard
the terrific roar of the breakers, and the dash of
the waves, as they broke over the deck.

"While we lay thus at the mercy of the waves,
I was comforted and supported by the captain's
child, a little girl, of eight or ten years old, who
was in the cabin with us. Her father came in
several times, during the lulls of the storm, to
see his child; and the sight of the captain is
always cheering in such a time of danger. As
the storm increased, I saw the little girl, rising
on her elbow and looking eagerly towards the
door, as if longing for her father's coming again.
He came at last. He was a large, rough, sailor-
looking man. He had on an immense coat,
great sea-boots, and an oil-skin cap, with flaps

hanging down his neck, streaming with water. He fell on his knees, on the floor, beside the low berth of his child, and stretched his arm over her, but did not speak.

"After a while he asked her if she was afraid. 'Father,' said the child, 'let me be with you, and I will not be afraid.'

"'With me,' he said, 'why, my child, you could not stand on the deck an instant.'

"'Father, do let me be with you,' she repeated.

"'My darling, you would be more frightened then,' he said, kissing her, while the tears were rolling down his rough weather-beaten cheeks.

"'No, father, I will not be afraid if I am only with you. O father! do let me be with you,' and she threw her arms round his neck, and clung fast to him. The strong man was overcome. He folded her in his arms, and wrapping his huge coat about her, carried her with him. The storm was howling dreadfully, but quiet as a lamb, that dear child knew no fear because she was nestling in her father's arms."

And when the child had left the cabin, the

lady passenger said to herself: "Let me learn a lesson from this child. She is not afraid in her father's arms. And have I no father? Is not God my Heavenly Father? Are not his everlasting arms round me? Then why should I be afraid?" This thought took away all her fear. She felt that God was with her, and found sweet peace and comfort in the thought, till the storm was over, and the vessel arrived safely at " the haven where they would be."

In this way we should acknowledge God's *presence.* This is the first point.

But secondly we should acknowledge God's — POWER, — as well as his presence.

We learn from the Bible that God's power is so great that he can do whatsoever he pleases. Nothing is impossible; nothing is too hard for the Lord. And all the power that God has he loves to make use of, to help his people when they have hard work to do, to strengthen them when they have heavy burdens to bear, and to comfort them when they have sore trials to pass through.

Look at David. When he went to fight the

lion, and the bear, who stole the kid from his flock, he acknowledged God's power by asking him to help him ; and he did so. And then when he came to fight the great giant, whose very appearance frightened the whole army of Israel, he did just the same thing. He told Saul, you remember, when Saul thought he was not strong enough for such a fight, how he fought and killed the lion and the bear. And then he said : " The God who delivered me out of the paw of the lion, and out of the paw of the bear, he will deliver me out of the hand of this Philistine." In this way David acknowledged God's power; and you know how God helped him.

And look at Shadrach, Meshech, and Abednego. Nebuchadnezzar said they must bow down and worship his graven image. They said they would not do it. The King threatened to throw them into the fiery furnace if they did not do it. They said their God was able to keep the fire from hurting them if he chose; but anyhow they would not worship a graven image. Thus, they acknowledged God's power, and you

all know how God protected and blessed them
for it.

And there are a great many instances out of
the Bible, in which God's people have acknowledged his power, and have been protected and
blessed by it.

In a large house, that stood in a lonely place,
in the south of England, there once lived a
lady and her two maid-servants. They were a
good way off from all other habitations; but
they trusted in God, and dwelt in peace and
safety. It was the lady's custom to go round
the house with her maids every evening, to see
that all the windows and doors were properly
fastened. One night she had been round with
them as usual, and seen that all was safe. The
servants left her in the entry, close to her room,
and then went to their own chamber, which was
quite at the other side of the house. As the
lady entered the room, she saw distinctly a man
hidden away under her bed. What could she
do? Her servants were far away. If she
screamed, they would not hear her; and, even if
they came to her help, what could three weak

women do against a desperate housebreaker! How then did she act? She felt that nothing but the power of God could save her. She lifted up her heart in silent prayer to God for help. Thus she acknowledged his power. She honored God by trusting him: we shall see directly how God honored her.

Quietly she closed the door, and locked it on the inside, as she was in the habit of doing. Then she leisurely brushed her hair, and, putting on her dressing-gown, she took her Bible, and sat down to read. She turned to the ninety-first Psalm, which speaks so beautifully of God's watchful care over his people by night and by day, and she read it aloud. Only think how sweet and comforting it must have been, as she read on, to feel as if God were speaking these precious words to her: "He that dwelleth in the secret place of the Most High shall abide under the shadow of the Almighty. He shall cover thee with his feathers, and under his wings shalt thou trust. Thou shalt not be afraid for the terror by night, nor for the arrow that flieth by day. Because thou hast made the Lord, even the Most High, thy habitation; there shall no evil befall thee, neither shall any plague come nigh thy dwelling. He shall call upon me, and I will answer him: I will be with him in trouble; I will deliver him, and honor him." When she had done reading, she knelt down and prayed, still uttering her words aloud. She committed herself, and her servants, to God's protection. She told him of their helplessness and dependence on him. She pleaded the promises she had just been reading in his blessed word, and prayed that she might find those promises fulfilled in her own experience. Then she put out the light, and lay down in bed; but she did *not* sleep.

A real brave and heroic woman she was. No soldier on the battle-field ever showed truer courage than she did. After a while she heard the robber come out from under the bed. He stood by her bedside. He spoke to her, and told her not to be frightened. Says he: "I came here to rob you; but, after the words you have read, and the prayers you have offered, nothing on earth would induce me to hurt you,

or touch a thing in your house.   But you must
remain perfectly quiet, and not attempt to in-
terfere with me.   I shall now give a signal to
my companions, which they will understand,
and then we will go away, and you may sleep
in peace, for I give you my solemn word that
no one shall harm you, and not the smallest
thing belonging to you shall be disturbed.   But,
before I go, you must give me the book you
read out of: I never heard such words before;
I must have that book."   She gave him her
Bible.   He then went to the window, and
whistled softly.   He returned to her bedside,
and said : " Now I am going.   Your prayer has
been heard, and no evil has befallen you."   He
left the room, and all was quiet.   The lady fell
asleep, in the sweet peace with which her trust
in God had filled her heart.

When the morning dawned and she awoke,
we may imagine how she poured out her
thanksgiving and praise to him who had " de-
fended " her " under his wings," and " kept " her
" safe under his feathers," so that she was not
" afraid of any terror by night."   The robber

proved true to his word, and not a thing in the house had been taken.

The lady heard nothing more of the robber for a number of years. One day, however, she was attending a Bible society meeting in a town in Yorkshire. After several clergymén had spoken, a man who was employed as . a colporteur of the society rose to speak. He told this story of the Lady and the Robber, in order to show the wonderful power of the Bible. He concluded by saying : "*I was that robber.*" The lady rose in the meeting, and said : "It's all true ; I am the lady," and sat down again.

But perhaps some of you may be ready to say : " Well, I've never been placed in danger like this, or had such an occasion of acknowledging God's power." Yes, but then you can acknowledge that power in little things, as well as in great things.

A minister was once trying to show his people the importance of acknowledging God's power by praying to him in trouble. Said he : "I knew a little boy, about thirty years ago, who had a sore hand. It became so bad that the doctor thought it would have to be cut off, to save the boy's life. On hearing this, the little boy went to a retired part of the garden, fell on his knees, and prayed God, for Jesus' sake, to save his poor hand. The next day, when the doctor came, he found the hand much better; and, a few days after, he said it would not be necessary to take it off. The boy lived to be a man; he became a minister;" and then, raising his hand, he said: "This is the hand. I hold it up before you, as a proof of the benefit of acknowledging God's power in prayer."

"Do you have any hard lessons to get?" said a gentleman one day, to a little school-girl.

"Yes, sir," she replied: "some of my lessons are very hard; but I pray to God to help me get them, and after I have prayed they seem easy."

That is the best way in the world to get hard lessons, or to do any thing else that is hard. I have found out, long ago, that it is the best way to make the writing of hard sermons easy.

Sometimes wicked people deny the power of God, and he makes them feel it in a dreadful way. There was a company of wood-cutters, some time ago, on the banks of the river Kennebec, in Maine.   They were talking one night of the danger to which they were exposed of being killed by the falling timber, as they were cutting trees in the forest.   One of them was an infidel.   "Nonsense!" said he, "I'm not afraid.   God Almighty isn't quick enough to kill me with a falling tree."

The next morning, he went out with his companions to work.   The first tree they went to work upon was a fine large one.   They have labored away on it for some time; it is nearly cut through; it begins to lean and crash; they stand aside; it comes thundering down; but, before it fairly reaches the ground, a branch, lodged on the top of a slender spruce, is hurled with fatal aim, as if by the hand of God; it strikes the infidel on the head; and, without a word, he falls to the ground a corpse.

"In all thy ways acknowledge him."   We should acknowledge *God's power.*

And then we should acknowledge God's — PROMISES.

The Bible is full of promises.   There are

promises here for the young, and promises for the old ; promises for the rich, and promises for the poor; promises for the sick, and promises for the well; promises for the living, and promises for the dying. The apostle Peter calls them " exceeding great and precious promises." They are all *sure* promises. When God gives them, he means just what he says in them. He never has broken one of these promises. He never will break them. And when we believe these promises, and live and act just as if we expected to find them fulfilled, then, we acknowledge God, so far as his promises are concerned.

Look at Jacob. He went away from his father's house, you remember, when he was a young man. The first night he spent on his journey he had an interesting dream. He saw a ladder, which reached from earth to heaven, and the angels of God were going up and down on it. God came to him in that dream, and said he would never leave him nor forsake him, but would keep him in all his journey, and bring him back, at last, in safety to his father's house.

That was God's promise to him. Jacob believed it; and years afterwards, when he was going back to his father's house, he was in great trouble. His brother Esau was angry with him, and came against him with an army of four hundred men to kill him. Jacob was greatly alarmed. He had no help but in God. He prayed earnestly to him. He reminded him of the promise given him years before, that he would bring him home again in safety. He pleaded with him to fulfil that promise, and to keep Esau from hurting him. God heard that prayer; he remembered his promise; he caused Esau's feelings to become entirely changed towards Jacob, so that, when he came up to him, instead of smiting him with the sword, as he had intended to do, he fell on his neck and kissed him, and was just as kind to him as he could be.

And God remembers his promises in just the same way now, and fulfils them, when his people acknowledge his promises, and pray to him in faith to fulfil them.

Not long ago, during a very dry summer,

some of the midland counties of England were suffering greatly for want of rain. Several pious farmers, who were afraid of losing their crops unless they should soon have rain, agreed with their minister, and others, to hold a special meeting at their church, for the purpose of praying for rain. They met accordingly, and the minister, coming early, had an opportunity of talking to some of the people before the meeting began. While he was thus engaged, he was surprised to see one of his little Sunday-school scholars walk into the church, staggering under the weight of a huge old family umbrella.

"Why, Mary, my child," he said, "what in the world made you bring that great umbrella on such a bright beautiful morning as this?"

The dear child looked up into his face, feeling surprised that a minister should ask such a question, and said: "Why, sir, as we are going to pray to God for rain, and God has promised to hear and answer his people when they pray, I thought I'd be sure to want the umbrella."

The minister felt reproved by the simple faith of this dear lamb. You see how this

child acknowledged God in regard to his promises. Well, shortly after, the meeting was
opened. While they were praying the wind
arose ; the sky, before so clear and bright,
became overcast with clouds; and soon, amidst
vivid flashes of lightning and heavy peals
of thunder, a storm of rain burst upon the
country. Those who came to the meeting
without properly acknowledging God's promises, and not expecting to receive the blessing
they came to ask for, had to take a soaking on
their way home for their want of faith, while
little Mary, and her minister, returned together
under the large old family umbrella.

Here is an example of a poor widow woman,
who was in great distress with her little ones,
but who acknowledged God's promises, and
obtained from him the help that she needed.
We may call it

THE WIDOW'S PRAYER.

In the winter of 1855, in the state of Iowa,
the snow fell early in November to the depth
of two feet. The storm was so great that

neither man nor beast could move against it. In a log cabin, six miles from the nearest house, lived a widow with four children: the oldest was eleven years of age, and the youngest a baby, only a year old. Her supply of food and fuel was very small, when the snow began falling. Day after day the stock melted away, until the fourth evening. Then the very last morsel of food was eaten for supper, and there was not wood enough left to keep the fire going for another day.

That night, according to her custom, she gathered her little ones around her, and read to them out of God's blessed book. Among the verses that she read were these words of the Psalmist: " I have been young, and now am old; yet have I not seen the righteous forsaken, nor his seed begging bread." " The lions do lack and suffer hunger, but they that wait on the Lord shall want no good thing." Then she kneeled down, with her helpless little ones, and prayed to God.

She told the Lord that their food was quite gone, and their fuel almost gone. She pleaded

the promises from his holy word which had just
been read.   She asked God to fulfil those
promises in this hour of their great need,
and to send them such help as they required.
She believed that these promises would be
fulfilled.   Then they went to bed and slept
soundly.

When the next morning dawned that mother
arose.   She kindled the fire and put the kettle
on, as she was in the habit of doing; although
now, for the first time in her life, she had
nothing to put in it.   But she felt sure that
something would come, because she believed
that God's promises never fail.

While she was waiting by the fire, a man in
a sleigh drove up to the house.   He knocked at
the door.   As soon as she opened it, he came in
and asked if they were in want of any thing.
Her heart was so full that it was some time
before she could speak.   But soon recovering
herself, she told him how they had eaten their
last morsel of food the night before, and then
had called on God to help them.

He was greatly surprised at what he heard.

Then he said to her, "Last night, about nine o'clock, my wife and I both had the thought come into our minds, that there was some one in this cottage needing help. We could hardly sleep any during the night for thinking about it. As soon as it was light this morning, I hastened to come out and inquire about it."

Then he went to his sleigh, and brought into the house bread, and flour, and meat, and groceries; and so the grateful mother had an abundant supply from which to prepare for her little ones a substantial breakfast, although they had gone to bed the night before without a particle of food in the house.

And during the day, the same kind-hearted person sent the poor widow a load of wood. And thus all her wants were supplied, by that God whom she had so truly acknowledged, by faith in his promises. And when we know that the person who brought this help was a stranger to the widow and her family, and when we see that the thought of sending this help came into his mind *at the very time when the*

distressed mother was crying to God for help, we
may be very sure that the thought did not
come there by chance, but *that God put it there,*
and that it was in this way he answered her
prayer for help. She had acknowledged God
in his promises, and so he fulfilled those promises by sending to her, in that unexpected
way, the help that was needed by herself and
little ones.

"In all thy ways acknowledge him."

We have seen that there are three things
about God we should acknowledge : these are,
his *presence,* his *power,* and his *promises.*

Let us remember these three *p*'s.

When Jesus was on earth he said to his disciples : "Without me ye can do nothing."
We cannot acknowledge him properly without
his help. Let us pray for his grace to help us,
and then, wherever we go, let us acknowledge
his presence, or carry the thought of him with
us. Let us acknowledge his power, by praying
for his help in all that we have to do. And let
us acknowledge his promises, by expecting and
praying to have them fulfilled for our relief

16

and comfort, whenever we are in trouble and sorrow.

I was reading lately of a dear little boy, only three years old, who beautifully practised the lesson which the text teaches. His mother had been out nearly all day, and came home at night, feeling very tired and unwell. She went early to bed to get a good night's rest. But the little boy was not tired at all, and disposed to talk a great deal. At last his mother said : " Charley, mamma is sick and tired, and can't talk to-night."

"Ma," said he, "God can make you well, can't he ? shall I ask him ? "

" Yes, my dear," said his mother.

Charley hopped up in bed, and kneeled down on the bed-clothes, and folding his little hands together offered this prayer : " O good heavenly Father, please to make my dear mamma well by morning for Jesus' sake." Then he crept back into bed, and in a few minutes he was asleep. When he awoke in the morning, his first question was : " Are you well this morning, mamma ? " Without thinking of what had taken place the night before, his mother said : " Yes, my dear, I am very well this morning." " Oh, I knew you would be," said Charley, clapping his hands for joy, " I knew you would be, for I prayed to God to make you well, and *Jesus always hears little children when they pray.*"

That is the kind of trust in God we ought all to have. Then, " in all our ways we shall acknowledge him." I will close my sermon with some sweet lines about trust in God.

> " Happy, Saviour, should I be,
> If I could but trust in thee ;
> Trust thy wisdom me to guide,
> Trust thy goodness to provide ;
> Trust thy saving health and power,
> Trust thee every day and hour ;
> Trust thee as the only light,
> In the darkest hour of night ;
> Trust in sickness, trust in health,
> Trust in poverty and wealth ;
> Trust in joy, and trust in grief,
> Trust thy promise for relief ;
> Trust thy blood to cleanse my soul,
> Trust thy grace to make me whole ;
> Trust thee living, dying too,
> Trust thee all my journey through.

Trust thee till my feet shall be
Planted on the crystal sea:
Trust thee, ever-blessed Lamb!
Till I wear the victor's palm;
Trust thee till my soul shall be
Wholly swallowed up in thee!"

IX.

THE CURE FOR CARE.

IX.

THE CURE FOR CARE.

" And Abraham called the name of the place Jehovah-Jireh." —
GENESIS xxii. 14.

THE place here spoken of, was that to which
Abraham went to offer up his son Isaac, as a
burnt-offering. Abraham was living, when this
took place, at Beersheba, in the southern part
of the land of Palestine. God came to him one
night, and told him to take his only son Isaac,
whom he loved, and offer him for a burnt-offering, on one of the mountains in the land of
Moriah, which he would show him. This was
a very hard thing, for a loving father to do with
his only son. But Abraham never hesitated.
He "rose up early in the morning," and went
to do what God had told him. After travelling
three days, they came to the place. It was
Mount Moriah to which God led him. This
was the hill around which the city of Jerusalem was afterwards built. Solomon made a

level place around this hill, and then built his temple over the top of it. People who visit Jerusalem now, can go and see this interesting spot. We had this pleasure during our stay in the Holy City. The mosque of Omar stands where Solomon's temple once stood. The beautiful rounded dome of that mosque — called the " Dome of the Rock" — rises directly over a great mass of rock, which is the top of Mount Moriah. I looked at that huge rock with great interest. As I stood gazing at it, I said to myself, — "There, on the top of that rock, is the very place to which Abraham came with his son Isaac. There he built an altar, and laid the wood in order upon it. There he bound Isaac, and laid him on the wood. There he took the knife to slay his son, and there, as he was holding that knife to his son's throat, God called to him from heaven. He told him not to slay his son, and showed him a ram caught by his horns in a thicket, which he was to offer as a sacrifice instead of his son."

What a relief to Abraham that must have been! Yes, and what a relief to Isaac too!

How glad he must have felt, when his father took him down from the altar, and unbound his limbs ! What thankfulness must have filled his heart, as he felt himself snatched from a sudden and painful death ! I thought I could see the happy boy, wiping the big drops of sweat from his brow, and looking around on every thing about him, as one would do who had never expected to see them again.

After such an experience as this, we do not wonder to find it said : "And Abraham called the name of the place Jehovah-Jireh." Jehovah means Lord. It is the most sacred name for God that the Bible tells us of. The word "Jireh" means will see, or will provide. And so Jehovah-Jireh means "the Lord will provide." One reason why all this was allowed to happen to Abraham on Mount Moriah, was to teach him how easily God can provide for his people, whatever is necessary for their help and comfort. And God has caused this interesting story to be written in the Bible, on purpose that we may learn the same lesson too. If we learn the lesson well that is taught us by these words, Jehovah-Jireh, the Lord will provide, it will be of great use to us. In going through this world, we all have a great many cares and troubles to meet. These are like heavy burdens that we have to bear. It is a great blessing to know, what is the best way of getting rid of these burdens, or if we cannot get rid of them, to find out how to bear them with the greatest ease and comfort. Nothing will help us to do this better than the words of our text, if we learn clearly to understand, and firmly to believe the lesson they teach.

This lesson is *the cure for care*, which the Bible furnishes. We are taught this lesson by the words which Abraham used when he said : " Jehovah-Jireh — the Lord will provide."

It will help us to learn this lesson, and to get rid of our care, if we remember three things that God provides for his people.

The first thing that God provides for his people is — PROTECTION IN DANGER.

It is wonderful how many illustrations we find, both *in* the Bible, and *out* of it, of the way in which God provides protection in danger for

his people. When we open the Bible for these
illustrations, they meet us everywhere. There
is the great ark, in which Noah and his family
were protected, from the deluge of water which
drowned the world. Look at it, as it goes floating
securely over the face of the troubled waters;
and it seems as though we could see "Jehovah-
Jireh, the Lord will provide," written in large
letters all over it. And when we turn from
this, and think of the tiny ark of bulrushes,
which floated on the quiet waters of the river
Nile, and protected the infant Moses from the
cruelty of Pharaoh, we see another illustration
of the same truth. And when we remember
how Joseph was protected from the wicked in-
tentions of his brethren; and how the whole
nation of the Israelites were protected from the
dangers of the wilderness, during the forty years
of their wanderings there; and how David was
protected for ten years while Saul was trying
in every way, to kill him; and how Jonah was
protected when thrown into the sea; how
Daniel was protected from the hungry lions,
and his three friends from the fierce flames of

the devouring furnace, — we see how full the
Bible is of illustrations of our text, "Jehovah-
Jireh — the Lord will provide."

But there are plenty of illustrations of this truth
to be found outside of the Bible. The animal and
the vegetable kingdom afford us plenty of illustrations of this same truth. Look at the scales of
the crocodile, and the thick, tough hide of the
rhinoceros, and the powerful trunk of the ele-
phant, and the strength and courage of the lion.
Look at the turtle, with the castle that it carries
about with it, and the snail crawling along with
its house on its back. When you see how God
provides for the protection of all these different
creatures, you see how each of them illustrates
the truth which Abraham was taught on Mount
Moriah, when he called the name of it —
Jehovah-Jireh.

A friend of mine has a very powerful microscope. The other day he showed me some
curious specimens through it. Among these
were some tiny little sea animals. They were
so small that they could not be seen with the
naked eye. They are made to live on the rocks

under the water; and, to protect themselves from being swept away by the force of the waves, they are furnished with the tiniest little limbs you ever saw. Each of these is made exactly in the shape of an anchor. This they fasten in the rock; and as I looked at them with wonder through the microscope, I thought: Why, even among these very little creatures we see Jehovah-Jireh too. The Lord provides for *their* protection.

And every apple, and pear, and peach, and plum that grows, shows the same thing, in the skin which is drawn over them for their protection. And so does every nut, in the hard shell which grows round its kernel. And so does every grain of wheat, and every ear of Indian-corn, in the coverings so nicely wrapped around them to keep them from harm.

And God is doing wonderful things all the time for the protection of his people.

A Christian sailor when asked why he remained so calm in a fearful storm, said, " If I fall into the sea, I shall only drop into the hollow of my Father's hand, for he holds all these waters there."

A lady was once riding in her carriage over a mountain road. She saw a beautiful flower springing up by the side of a great rock. She got down from her carriage, and thought she would take up the little flower, and plant it in her green-house. But, small and delicate as that flower was, she found it impossible to remove it, because its roots ran under the great rock, by whose side it grew. And as she took her seat in her carriage again, she thought to herself, "Just so Jesus — the Rock of ages — shelters those who trust in him." And that little rock-protected flower seemed, as it grew in its beauty, to be saying to all who went by, — "Jehovah-Jireh."

Little Bessie was in bed. Nurse came in, and found her lying wide awake.

"All alone in the dark!" said nurse, "and not afraid at all : are you, Bessie, darling?"

"No, indeed," said Bessie, "for I'm not all alone. God is here. I look out of the window, and see the stars ; and God seems to be looking down on me, with all his eyes."

"To be sure," said nurse, "but God is up in the sky, a great way off."

" No," said Bessie, " God is here too, and sometimes he seems to be *clasping me in his arms*, and then I feel so happy."

That little child might go to sleep saying, — " Jehovah-Jireh, the Lord will provide," for my protection.

A young widow, with two children, was living in the city of Berlin. She was a Christian woman, and trusted in Jehovah-Jireh to take care of her. One evening she had to be away from home for a while. During her absence, a man entered her house, for the purpose of robbing her. But " the Lord who provides" protected her from this danger, in a very singular way. On returning to her room, she found a note lying on her table, which read as follows : —

" Madam, — I came here with the intention of robbing you; but the sight of this little room, with the religious pictures hanging round it, and those two sweet-looking children, quietly sleeping in their little bed, have touched my heart. I cannot take any thing of yours. The small amount of money lying on your desk, I

leave untouched, and I take the liberty of add-
ing fifty dollars besides." [1]

The Bible tells us that " the hearts of men are
in the hands of God, and he turneth them as
the rivers of water are turned." He turned the
heart of this robber from his wicked purpose,
and in this way he protected the widow who
trusted in him.

One morning a Christian farmer, in Rhode
Island, put two bushels of rye in his wagon, and
started to the mill to get it ground. On his
way to the mill he had to drive over a bridge,
that had no railings to the sides of it. When
he reached the middle of this bridge, his horse,
a quiet, gentle creature, began, all at once to
back. In spite of all the farmer could do, he
kept on backing, till the hinder wheels went
over the side of the bridge, and the bag of grain
was tipped out, and fell into the stream. Then
the horse stood still.

Some men came to help the farmer. The
wagon was lifted back, and the bag of grain
fished up from the water. Of course it could
not be taken to the mill in that state. So the

farmer had to take it home and dry it. He had prayed that morning that God would protect and bless him through the day, and he wondered what this accident had happened for. He found out, however, before long.

On spreading out the grain to dry, he noticed a great many small pieces of glass mixed up with it. If this had been ground up with the grain into flour, it would have caused the death of himself and his family. But Jehovah-Jireh was on that bridge. He made the horse back, and throw the grain into the water, to save that family, from the danger that threatened them.

Protection in danger is one thing that God will provide for his people. The recollection of this should help to cure care, or to keep us from being too anxious.

" Jehovah-Jireh — the Lord will provide."

The second thing that God provides for his people is — RELIEF IN TROUBLE.

There are many troubles that we meet with as we go on through life, and in which no one can give us such relief as God can. Sometimes

17

people are in trouble, because they want to get information, in regard to something on which their comfort depends, and God is the only one who can provide relief for them, by giving them the information which they need.

Here is a striking illustration of the way in which God can provide this relief, when it is needed. Some years ago, there was a Christian man in England, who was in trouble. He was poor, and suffered much for want of money. A valuable property had been left to him. It would be sufficient to make him comfortable all the rest of his life, if he could only get possession of it. But in order to do this, it was necessary to find out some deeds connected with this property. But neither he, nor any of his friends, could tell where those deeds were to be found. They had tried to find them for a long time; but all their efforts had been in vain. At last, God provided relief for this man in his trouble in a very singular way.

On one occasion, Bishop Chase, who was then the Bishop of the Protestant Episcopal church in Ohio, was on a visit to the city of Philadelphia. He was stopping at the house of Mr. Paul Beck. One day, while staying there, he received a letter from one of the Bishops of the Church of England. This letter was written to Bishop Chase, to ask him to make some inquiries about the deeds relating to the property of which we have spoken. The letter had been sent out first to Ohio, and then to Washington, where the Bishop had been. From there it had been sent on after him to Philadelphia. If Bishop Chase had received this letter in Ohio, or in Washington, he would probably have read it, and then have said to himself: "I can't find out any thing about these deeds," and would have written to his friend, the English Bishop, telling him so. But the letter came to him while he was at Mr. Beck's house. Mr. Beck was present when the letter was received. The Bishop read it to him. When Mr. Beck heard the letter read, he was very much astonished. "Bishop Chase," said he, "it is very singular that this letter should have come to you while you are at my house. Sir, I am the only man in the world, that can give you the information asked for in this letter. I have the deeds in my possession. I have had them for more than forty years, and never could tell what to do with them, or where to find the persons to whom they belong." How wonderful it was that this letter, after coming across the ocean, and going from one place to another in this country, should reach the Bishop while he was in the house, and in the presence of the only man in the world who could tell about those lost deeds! And if the poor man to whom the property belonged, when he came into possession of it, knew about the singular way in which those deeds were found, he certainly would have been ready to write upon them, in big round letters, the words: "Jehovah-Jireh — the Lord will provide." God provided relief for him in his trouble.

"Mother, I think God always hears when we scrape the bottom of the barrel," said a little boy to his mother one day. His mother was poor. They often used up their last stick of wood, and their last bit of bread before they could tell where the next supply was to come from. But they had so often been provided for in unexpected ways, just when they were most in need, that the little boy thought, "*God always heard when they scraped the bottom of the barrel.*" This was only that little fellow's way of saying, what Abraham said when he called the name of the place, where God had delivered him, Jehovah-Jireh.

Here is an illustration of the way in which God sends relief in trouble. The story is told by the Christian woman, to whom it happened, in her own language.

"About the month of January, 1863, I was living in Connecticut, alone, with two little boys, one of them four years old, and the other about a year and a half old. My husband was away in the service of his country. When the coldest weather came, I was nearly out of wood. I went down into the village one day to try and get some, but tried in vain. So many men were away in the army that help was scarce. Very little wood was brought into market, and those living on the main street got all that came ; while those who lived outside the village could get none. I tried to buy a quarter of a

cord from two or three merchants, but could
not get any. One of them told me he could
not get what he wanted for his own family.
Another said he was not willing to yoke up his
team for so small a quantity; but, as I only had
a dollar and seventy-five cents, I could not buy
any more, and so I was obliged to go home without any.

"I went back to my little ones, feeling very
sad. But while I sat there almost ready to cry,
the words of Abraham came into my mind,
— 'Jehovah-Jireh — the Lord will provide.'
Then I went up to my chamber. There I
kneeled down and told God of my trouble, and
asked him to help me, and send the relief that
we needed. Then I went to the window, and
waited, looking down the street, expecting to
see the wood coming. After waiting a while,
without seeing any come, my faith began to
fail. I said to myself, — 'The Lord did provide
for Abraham, but he won't provide for me.' Our
last stick of wood was put in the stove. It was
too cold to keep the children in the house without fire. I got their clothes out, and thought I

would take them to the house of a kind neighbor, where I knew they could stay till we got some wood. But, just as I was going out with the children, in passing by the window, I saw the top of a great load of wood, coming up the road, towards our little house. 'Can that be for us?' I asked myself. Presently I saw the wagon turn off the road, and come up towards our door. Then I was puzzled to know how to pay for it. A dollar and seventy-five cents, I knew, would only go a little way towards paying for all that wood. The oxen came slowly on, dragging the load to our door. I asked the man if there was not some mistake about it. 'No, ma'am,' said he, 'there is no mistake.'

"'I didn't order it, and I can't pay for it?' was my reply.

"'Never mind, ma'am,' said he, 'a friend ordered it, and it is all paid for.'

"Then he unhitched the oxen from the wagon, and gave them some hay to eat.

"When this was done, he asked for a saw and axe, and never stopped till the whole load was cut and split, and piled away in the wood-shed.

"This was more than I could stand. My feelings overcame me, and I sat down and cried like a child. But these were not bitter tears of sorrow. They were tears of joy and gladness, of gratitude and thankfulness. I felt ashamed of myself for doubting God's word, and I prayed that I might never do so again. What pleasure I had in using that wood! Every stick of it, as I took it up, seemed to have a voice with which to say — Jehovah-Jireh. As Abraham stood on the top of Mount Moriah he could say, — 'The Lord *will* provide,' but every day as I went into our wood-shed, I could point to that blessed pile of wood, sent from heaven, and say, — 'The Lord *does* provide.' "

A mother one morning gave her two little ones, books and toys, to amuse them, while she went upstairs to attend to something. A half-hour passed quietly away, and then one of the little ones went to the foot of the stairs, and, in a timid voice, called out: "Mamma, are you there?"

"Yes, darling!" "All right," said the little
one, and went on with her play. By and by
the question was repeated, "Mamma, are you
there?" "Yes, darling." "All right," said the
child again, and once more went on with her
play. And this is just the way we should feel
towards Jesus. He has gone upstairs, to the
right hand of God, to attend to some things for
us. He has left us down in the lower room of
this world, to be occupied here for a while.
But to keep us from being worried by fear,
or care, he speaks to us from his word, as
that mother spoke to her little ones. He says
to us: "Fear not: I am with thee." "I will
never leave thee, nor forsake thee." "Jehovah-
Jireh — the Lord will provide." The second
thing that the Lord will provide is relief in
trouble. And the recollection of this will help
to cure care for us.

*But there is a third thing that the Lord will
provide, and that is* — SALVATION FOR THE
SOUL.

And this should have a great influence in
curing care with us. The soul is the most

valuable thing we have. Jesus said that if a man should gain the whole world, and lose his soul, he would make a foolish bargain. And Jesus knows what the real value of the soul is, better than any one else. He made the soul. And when it was lost, he paid the price that was necessary to redeem it. And when we come to understand the value of the soul, we shall never have any peace or comfort till we know that it is safe. The thought of losing the soul will fill us with care and anxiety. This care will become a burden to us, and we never shall find relief from this burden till we hear the voice of Jesus, saying: "Come unto me, all ye that labor, and are heavy laden, and I will give you rest."

Here is an illustration of a man who was very much burdened with care on account of his soul, and who had this care cured by the salvation which Jesus provides. Many years ago there was a very celebrated preacher, whose name was the Rev. George Whitefield. He went travelling all over England, and this country, preaching the gospel, and did a great deal of good in this way. One day a brother of Mr. Whitefield's heard him preach. The sermon led him to see what a sinner he was, and he became very sorry on account of his sins. He was burdened with care because he thought his soul could not be saved. And for a long time it seemed as if he could get no relief from this burden. And the reason of it was that he was not willing to believe the word of Jesus. It is only in this way that we can be saved. When we read the promises of Jesus, in the Bible, we must believe that he means just what he says. We must trust his word, and then we shall be saved.

Well, one evening this brother of Mr. Whitefield, was taking tea with the Countess of Huntingdon. This was an earnest Christian lady, who took a great interest in all good ministers, and the work they did for Jesus. She saw that the poor man was in great trouble of mind, and she tried to comfort him, as they took their tea, by talking to him about the great mercy of God to poor sinners, through Jesus Christ.

" Yes, my lady," said the sorrowful man, " I know what you say is true.   The mercy of God is infinite.   I am satisfied of this.   But, ah ! my friend, there is no mercy for me.   I am a wretched sinner, a *lost* man."

" I am glad to hear it, Mr. Whitefield," said Lady Huntingdon. " I am glad in my heart that you have found out you are a lost man."

He looked at her with great surprise. " What, my lady !" he exclaimed, " glad, did you say ? glad at heart that I am a lost man ? "

" Why, certainly I am, Mr. Whitefield, " said she, " for you know, Jesus Christ came into the world, to ' seek and to save them that are lost.' And if you feel that you are a lost man, why you are just one of those that Jesus came to save."

This remark had a great effect on Mr. Whitefield.   He put down the cup of tea that he was drinking, and clapped his hands together, saying, — " Thank God for that.   Thank God for that."   He believed God's promise then.   That cured his care.   It took away his trouble.   It saved his soul.   He was taken suddenly ill, and died that same night, but he died happy.

Here is another illustration of the way in which Jesus saves people, for doing nothing else, but simply trusting in him. It was given by a minister who was settled in the coal region, and had a good deal to do with miners. He was talking one day with a hard-working miner, on the subject of religion. The man had never joined the church, but he was so correct in his conduct, that the minister felt sure he must be a Christian. He asked the man if he thought he was a Christian, and what reason he had for thinking so. This was the honest miner's answer: —

" Sir," said he, " you know I am no scholar, but I'll tell you the best way I can why I hope I am a Christian.

" It is not what *I* do that I trust in, but what Christ has done for me. You've been down the shaft into the mine, sir. This will help me to tell you what I mean. For a long time I was trying to do what was right: to live as I ought to; and so was trusting to my own works for salvation. But all the while I felt as if I was still down at the bottom of the shaft.

All I could do didn't get me out of the pit.
Then God showed me that all my righteousness
was but filthy rags, as the Bible says.   But how
was I to get out of the shaft ?   Why, at last I
found that the only way out of the deep mine,
into which sin had brought us, was to do just as
I do when I want to get out of the coal mine.
To do this, I have only to get into the bucket
when it comes down, and trust to the men at
the windlass to draw me out.   And so I find it
is about my soul.   I can't draw myself out of
the pit ; but I trust in Jesus, and leave it all to
him.   I used to try to do what was right, and
to serve God, because I was afraid of him and
of the judgment; but now I try to serve
and please God, because I love him."

This shows us very clearly the way in which
God provides salvation for his people.

Here is another illustration of the same truth.
A minister was once visiting an old man, who
was in great distress and trouble about the salvation of his soul.   He had just the same difficulty that the miner had, as mentioned in the
last story.   He thought he must work himself

out of the shaft: he was not willing just to put himself in the bucket, and trust to the men at the windlass to get him out.

At last the minister said to him: "Now, suppose I should go to a shop, and buy something for you, and pay for it, and tell you to go and get it; would it be necessary to take any money with you?"

"No," said the old man, brightening up: "it would be paid for."

"Need you make any promises to pay at some future time?" asked the minister.

"No," he replied: "I should have it for nothing."

"Well, it is just so," said the minister, "with the forgiveness of sins, and the salvation of the soul. Jesus has paid the full price for us. The groans, the sighs, the tears, the wrath, the pain, the punishment our sins deserved, he took upon himself; he bore it all; he paid the full price for our salvation. He bought it for us with his precious blood, and he offers it to us, as the Bible says, 'without money, and without price.'"

" Yes," said the old man, as his eyes filled with tears : " I see it now, though I never saw it before.   It is pardon for nothing ; salvation for nothing.   Now I understand what the apostle means when he says, ' Eternal life is the *gift* of God, through Jesus Christ our Lord.'   Jesus paid for it, and now God gives it to us *all for nothing*."

There is just one other story I wish to tell, and this shows us how quickly God can save the soul when he pleases to do so.   A Christian father and mother had long prayed for their son, that he might become a Christian and be saved.   But it seemed as if their prayers were not to be heard.   He grew up to be a careless, obstinate, disobedient boy ; and, at last, he ran away from home, and became a sailor.

One day, on board the ship, he had mounted up the rigging, and, while there, lost his hold, and fell overboard.   A boat was lowered at once to pick him up ; but, as the vessel was going very fast at the time, it was a good while before the young man could be reached.   At last, however, he was brought on board, though he seemed to be in a lifeless state. The surgeon of the ship used all the means he could to restore him, but all seemed to be in vain. His comrades had given up all hope of saving him, when he gave some signs of life. Then they renewed their efforts, and after a while the young man opened his eyes, and cried out, in tones of joy : " *Jesus Christ has saved me !* "

Then he was silent again, and it was a good while before he could tell what he had felt, in his fall, and while he was struggling in the water. After he was quite recovered, he gave this account of himself : —

" While falling from the yard-arm, as soon as I felt my danger, it seemed as if all the sins of my life stood before me, as quick as the lightning's flash. I saw what a dreadful sinner I was. I was afraid of death, and the punishment to follow. Then this text of Scripture came into my mind ; I had often heard my father repeat it : ' *This is a faithful saying, and worthy of all acceptation, that Jesus Christ came into the world to save sinners.*' I lifted my heart to him with the earnest cry, ' Lord Jesus, save me !' He

18

heard my cry: my sins are pardoned; I am saved. I thank God for that fall!"

The result showed that he was sincere. From that day onward he lived a new life. He returned to his parents, and became their support and comfort for the rest of their lives.

The Bible tells us that Jesus is "able to save unto *the uttermost* those who come unto God through him." How wonderful his power is, to be able to save a man's soul while falling from the yard-arm into the water!

This story may well comfort parents and teachers, and keep them from being discouraged when they see no fruit from their labors.

And so we have a good cure for care in these precious words: "Jehovah-Jireh — the Lord will provide." And when we remember the three things that he provides, — protection from danger; relief in trouble; and salvation for the soul, — we see that there is no reason why we should be much troubled about any thing, if we only have Jesus, who is Jehovah-Jireh, as our friend.

X.

THE HEAVENLY BREAD.

X.

THE HEAVENLY BREAD.

" I am the living bread which came down from heaven."
JOHN vi. 51.

BREAD is the most useful of all things. We call it "the staff of life," because we have to depend upon it so much. We can get along without almost any thing, easier than we can get along without bread. Jesus is like bread indeed; but not like common bread. He says of himself: "I am the *living* bread that came down from heaven." Heavenly things are better than earthly things. And the " living bread that comes down from heaven," is better than any other bread.

Every thing that we find in Jesus, is better than what we find in others. You know that we value the different things around us, according to the material out of which they are made. Some things are made of wood, like our chairs and tables; some are made of clay, like the dishes we use every day; some are made of stone, like the steps at our doors, and the walls of some of our houses; some are made of iron, like our knives, and tools, our locomotives, and the rails on which they run; some are made of brass, or copper, or bronze, like many of our mantle ornaments; some are made of silver, like our beautiful tea-sets; and some are made of gold, like our watch-chains and cases, our rings and jewels. And the things that are golden we consider the most valuable, and the best of all. But Jesus is golden, and glorious in all that belongs to him. When Moses was speaking of him, he said: "His work is perfect" (Deut. xxxii. 4). And so in the language of the hymn we may well ask the question: —

"Oh, who is like Jesus?"

There is none like Jesus, in heaven above, or on the earth beneath. And so there is no bread like that which he gives to all who love him. He says: "I am the living bread, which came down from heaven."

And the subject which these words give us to speak about is, —

Jesus the Heavenly Bread.

And there are *three* things which this heavenly bread does for us, which show us how well Jesus may be compared to it.

The first thing that this heavenly bread does for us when we eat it is, that it — MAKES US GOOD.

And remember that, when we are learning about Jesus, and believing in him, and loving him, then we are eating this heavenly bread. And one effect of our eating it will be that it will make us good. And it is only by eating this bread that we can be made good. If we do not eat this bread we cannot be good. Jesus came down from heaven as "the living bread," on purpose to make us good. Sometimes when persons are speaking to the young, we hear them say: "You must be good, or else Jesus will not love you." But this is a mistake. The Bible tells us that "there is none righteous, none that doeth good; no, not one" (Rom. iii. 10, 12). If we had "to be good," or make ourselves good before Jesus would love us, then, it is very sure, he would not love us at all, for we never could make ourselves good. The Bible teaches us that Jesus loved us, and came to help and save us, just because we were sinners; weak, and miserable, and unable to help ourselves, or make ourselves better. Jesus does not love our sins. He hates them, and wants to have them put away. But he loves *us*, although we are sinners, and he wishes us to come to him, on purpose that our sins may be pardoned, and put away, and that he may make us good. And there is nothing in the world, but learning about Jesus, and loving him, or eating this heavenly bread, that can really make us good. But *this* will do it. It never fails to produce this result.

Now let us look at some examples of the way in which people are made good by eating this heavenly bread.

THE BEST BOOK.

Some years ago, a person who was an infidel,
went into a bookstore in this city, and said to
the bookseller : —

" Have you got ' Paine's Age of Reason,' sir ? "

Thomas Paine, the author of this book, was
an infidel, and he wrote this book on purpose
to ridicule the Bible. It is full of ignorant and
wicked things against the Bible, and was written
for the purpose of keeping people from reading
God's blessed book.

The bookseller was a good Christian man.
Nothing in the world would have induced him
to keep such a book, as that which had just been
asked for. He started a little at this question.
Then he looked at the stranger with pity, and
finally said : —

" No, sir: I don't keep that book. But I
have the best book ever published in Philadelphia. If you will promise to read it, I will
gladly lend you a copy of it."

The idea of reading the *best book* in the city,
and that, too, without costing him any thing,

seemed very pleasant to the stranger, who was very fond of reading; and, without hesitation, he gave the promise.

The bookseller then handed him a Bible. The man looked vexed; for, being an infidel, he hated the Bible. But he was a truthful man; and so, feeling bound by his promise, he took the Bible home with him, and read it carefully through. God blessed the reading of his word to that man's soul. As he read on he was led to see that he was a sinner. Then he began to pray to Jesus. His infidelity left him, and he became a humble believer in Jesus, and one of his loving friends and followers. He returned the Bible to the bookseller with many thanks, and bought a copy for himself. Eating of this heavenly bread made a good Christian of the man who had been an infidel before.

WHY EVERY THING WENT WRONG.

A poor lame boy had been converted in Springfield, Massachusetts. His home had been a very unhappy one, and he had been very unhappy in it. He went to the minister, whose services he attended, to talk with him about joining the church. In the course of their conversation he said to the minister : " Once every thing went wrong at our house. Father was wrong, and mother was wrong, and sister was wrong ; but since I have learned to love and serve Jesus, it's very different. I know now how it was that every thing went wrong before. It was *because I was wrong myself.*"

Yes, if we only get things straightened out between our own hearts and God, it will be a wonderful help to us in getting on comfortably with those about us. This poor boy had learned to eat the heavenly bread, and he felt that it had put things right within him. It had made him good.

A NEW TESTAMENT SPOILING A DOG.

Mr. Moffatt, the celebrated missionary of Southern Africa, and the father-in-law of the famous Dr. Livingstone, tells a story which shows, in a ludicrous way, what the Africans thought about the power of this heavenly bread to do good to those who ate it.

A poor African came to Mr. Moffatt, one day, with a very sad face. He looked as though he had met with some great loss. "What's the matter," asked Mr. Moffatt.

"You know that good dog that I had to take care of my sheep. He was so useful to me in guarding them, and so bold and fierce in driving off the wild beasts that came to devour the sheep, but now he is spoiled."

"How so?" asked the missionary; "what has happened to him?"

"Why, he has torn my New Testament to pieces, and eaten some of the leaves."

"Never mind," said Mr. Moffatt, "you shall have another Testament."

"Thank you, sir, for that; but what shall I do about the dog? He was so fierce and good at fighting. But the New Testament is full of love and gentleness, and after the dog has eaten some of its leaves, it will take all the fight out of him, and spoil him for taking care of sheep."

Mr. Moffatt told the man that it was not eating the leaves of the Testament that would have this effect, but understanding, and believing, and trying to do what it teaches, and that his dog would have as much fierceness and fight in him as ever, although he had eaten some of the leaves of the Testament. This poor man was very ignorant, but he had great faith in the power of the heavenly bread to make those good who eat it.

RELIGION TAKES THE MAD OUT OF PEOPLE.

Lucy was a little girl, about five years old. She was in the infant school connected with the church which her mother attended. Lucy's father was a man of a very violent temper, and was not a member of the church, though he attended occasionally. He had had a quarrel with one of his neighbors, and would not speak to him, or say any thing about him except what was bad.

It happened that there was a revival of religion, in the village where Lucy lived, and her father and his neighbor, whom he considered as his enemy, both became Christians about the same time. The first occasion of their meeting together after this change had taken place, was on coming home from church one Sunday. They shook hands warmly. Each said he was sorry for what he had done, and asked the other to forgive him. Lucy walked on, feeling very glad for what she had seen and heard. When she reached home, she said to her mother: —

"Mother, what a nice thing religion is, because *it takes the mad out of people.*"

This is true. If we really eat of the heavenly bread, it will have just this effect on us.

VADIVALU, THE HINDOO THIEF.

Some time ago, in the district of Tinnevelly, in India, there was a gang of robbers. The leader, or chief of the band, was named Vadivalu. He was a very bad man, and everybody, in all the country round, was afraid of him. All the robbery and mischief done, for miles around, could be traced to him and his followers. He was always ready for any evil work. To burn, to rob, to kill, or do any other evil thing, was just what he delighted in. But though the villagers sometimes employed this man to do work for them, they dreaded him.

If they were travelling alone, or in the dark, it was a common saying that they would rather meet a cobra-capella, — their most poisonous serpent, — than Vadivalu. And this was saying a great deal.

Now let us see what effect eating of the heavenly bread had on this bad man.

One day, Vadivalu was passing by the mission station of Palamcotta, with some cattle, when one of his bullocks was hurt, and he was obliged to wait till it could be cured. While he was waiting here, a Christian woman connected with the mission, and who knew about his life, ventured to tell him that his evil ways would lead him to destruction, but that if he would ask Jesus Christ to forgive him, and make his heart clean, he would be saved. He did not seem to notice her words much; but while he remained at Palamcotta, he went to hear the missionary preach several times. The words that he heard had a great effect on him. He saw what a great sinner he had been. He cried earnestly for mercy, and God heard and answered his prayers.

When he came back to Tinnevelly, and said that he was a Christian, you can imagine the surprise of all who had known him. Many would not believe it. But when he went to the missionary, and told him what God had done for his soul, he was satisfied. And when the great robber was baptized, and joined the church, everybody wondered, but everybody was glad.

And then they watched him to see how he would act. For some of the people said they did not believe that any man, who had so long lived such an idle life of robbery and wrong, would ever be willing to settle down, and live like a Christian. But they were mistaken.

Vadivalu was thoroughly changed. He that had stolen, stole no more. The bold, bad man, the man of violence, and wrong, and robbery, and bloodshed, became honest, and industrious, and kind, and gentle, and loving, and true. Like the man, out of whom Jesus cast the evil spirits, those who came to see him found him "changed and in his right mind, sitting at the feet of Jesus." He who had been a plague and curse to all the country round, became a comfort and a blessing. The last thing that was heard of this man was, that he was taking his little grandchild to church, that he might learn about the Saviour; "for, surely," said he, "if God has had mercy on me, — the greatest sinner in Tinnevelly, — won't he have mercy on this dear little one?"

And all these examples show us, how well Jesus may be called the heavenly bread, because eating of this bread — *makes us good.*

But, in the second place, Jesus may be called the heavenly bread, because eating of this bread — MAKES US GREAT.

When our Saviour was on earth, he said one day, in speaking about great men, that John the Baptist was the greatest man that ever lived. Most people do not think so. If you ask those who are not Christians, to make out a list of the names of the greatest men the world has known, you will find that, foremost on the list, they will put such names as — Alexander the Great, Julius Cæsar, and Napoleon Bonaparte, and men of that class; but you will not find the names of men like John the Baptist among them. But Jesus understands, much better than we do, what true greatness is, and who are really great men. And he did not make a mistake when he said that John the Baptist was one of the greatest men that ever lived. But he was speaking of greatness in the sight of God, and not of greatness in the sight of men. God considers those the greatest who know him, and love him, and serve him the best. And it was because John the Baptist did this so well, that Jesus put him foremost among the great ones of the earth. And just so far as we learn to do this, God will call us great, and we shall be great indeed. But if we fail of doing this, however great men may call us, we never shall be great in God's sight.

And Jesus may well be called the heavenly bread, because, if we eat this bread, or, which is the same thing, if we learn to know, and love, and serve him, it will make us great in the sight of God.

Let us look at some examples of those who have eaten of this heavenly bread, and been made great by it.

PITY AND FORGIVE.

Not long ago, two boys, who belonged to the same Sunday school, were playing one Saturday in a house that was being repaired. One of the boys, named John, was trying to be a Christian. He had begun to eat the heavenly bread. The other boy, named Charley, was a careless boy, and felt no interest in the things of which the Bible speaks. In the midst of their play, Charley very thoughtlessly threw a handful of dust and lime into Johnny's face. Some of the lime got into his eyes, and gave him great pain. For a time he could not see at all, and they were afraid he might lose his sight. When the poor boy went home and told his father, he was very angry.

Not being a Christian man, he swore that the next time he met Charley, he would throw him into the canal. Johnny was sorry to hear his father say this, and though suffering great pain from the effects of the lime, he said : —

"No, father, don't do that. Let's forgive him, and pity him for not having more sense."

That was real noble in Johnny, and his father *felt* it to be so. It made him ashamed of what he had said; and, of course, he never carried out his threat. Eating the heavenly bread had made Johnny great in spirit.

GOOD FOR EVIL.

"I shan't do it," said little Danny, to his sister Nettie, as they were playing with the blocks, and doubling his fist he struck her in the face.

Nettie started with surprise. Her cheeks grew red. Her eyes flashed with anger, and she was on the point of hitting her brother back. But, just at that moment, she thought of the text she had repeated to her teacher on the previous Sunday. It was this: "Be not overcome of evil, but overcome evil with good."

Nettie had not fully understood the meaning of it at that time. But she had been thinking a great deal about it since Sunday. She prayed God to help her understand the meaning of this verse, and then to do what it teaches. At last she saw clearly what it meant.

"Yes, that's it," she said to herself. "It means, as aunt Dolly told me last Christmas, that when I want to pull Danny's hair, because he pulls mine, I must n't do it, but must 'overcome evil with good' by being kind to him instead. And so, by God's help, I'll try to do the very next time Danny treats me bad."

This was a good resolution, and Nettie bore it in mind for several days; but somehow it seemed as if Danny would not be provoking. And now, just when she was least expecting it, the temptation to evil came upon her so strong, that before she had time to think she had almost struck her brother.

But she did not do it. She remembered her text. A silent prayer went up, — "Lord, help me to do right;" and then leaning forward, and putting her soft white hands on Danny's cheek, she kissed him right on the mouth.

And now it was Danny's turn to be surprised. He had expected a blow, in return for the one he had given, and he was prepared for that. But a gentle, loving kiss, in return for his blow, was something he was not prepared for. He looked at his sister a moment, and his eyes filled with tears as he said : —

"Forgive me, Nettie, and I 'll never hit you again."

"All right, Danny," said the dear child. "This is what the Bible means by overcoming evil with good."

Nettie is in heaven now, and Danny has grown to be a man. He is a good Christian man, and a Sunday-school teacher. He loves to tell the scholars about his sister Nettie, and the lesson she taught him, about overcoming evil with good. And he always winds up by saying: "Ah! if my sister Nettie had lived she would have been a *great woman;* for Solomon says : 'He that ruleth his own spirit, is greater than he that taketh a city.'" (Prov. xvi. 32.) But it was eating of the heavenly bread that taught Nettie how to be great.

I met with a good illustration of this point of our subject, in a recent number of an English missionary periodical. The incident to which it refers, occurred not long ago, in connection with one of the English missionary stations in New Guinea, Australia.   It is headed —

AN ADVENTURE IN TORRES STRAITS.

Torres Straits is the name given to the channel of water, that runs between the Island of New Guinea, and the Island, or Continent of Australia or New Holland.

A large fishing-boat left Cape York, at the entrance of Torres Straits, to go up the straits on a fishing voyage. The party in the boat consisted of four persons, — two white men, a native boy, and a lad from one of the Loyalty Islands, who was called by the white men, " Billy." This boy had attended the Mission School, and there had learned to know and love Jesus. He had eaten of the heavenly bread, and we shall see, directly, how it had made him great. They had not gone very far on their voyage, before the boat was upset. They found it was impossible to get the boat righted. There was no one in sight to help them, and all that they could do, was to cling to the boat, and be drifted hither and thither, just as the wind and tide might carry them.

Every thing in the boat was lost; and so they had neither water to drink, nor food of any kind to eat. Billy, like most of the South-Sea islanders, felt at home in the water, and could swim almost like a fish. It would have been an easy thing for him to have swung off from the boat, and have swum to the nearest land. But none of his companions knew how to swim, and he chose rather to stay with them, and share their dangers and trials, whatever they might be.

They drifted about for *sixteen hours*, and then were cast ashore on an island called Hoody Island. But, on looking round here, they found that there was neither water, nor provisions of any kind on the island. So they were not much better off here, than when drifting about on the capsized boat. Unless something could be done, they must soon perish on land, although saved from death by drowning. The nearest point from which help could be had, was an island three miles and a half distant. But how was that to be reached! They had lost their oars and could not manage the boat. Billy was the only one in the little company who could swim. After talking it all over with the captain, he bravely made up his mind to try and swim to that island. This was a great undertaking. Just think of it! He had been drifting about in the water for sixteen hours, without any thing to eat or drink. And now, he was going to try and swim between three and four miles, and that, too, against a strong tide that was running at the rate, as the sailors say, of three and a half knots an hour.

They kneeled down and prayed that God would help him. Then Billy got ready for his long swimming voyage. He shook hands with them all, and said to the captain: —

"Suppose me catch land, me see you again; suppose me no catch land, good-bye." Then he plunged into the water, and struck out towards the distant land. His companions watched him till he was out of sight; and then they sat down to wait, and wonder whether the brave boy would ever come back again.

But he did come back. The God in whom he trusted gave him strength to keep on swimming and floating, till he reached the island, or, as he expressed it, till he was able to " catch the land." And when he came back with help, to save his friends from death, they overwhelmed him with their thanks. But Billy stopped them by saying : " You no thank me. Thank God. God, he do it all."

Here we have a fine illustration of the greatness that comes from eating this heavenly bread. Jesus may well be called the heavenly bread, because this bread makes us — great.

But there is a third reason why Jesus may be called the heavenly bread, and that is that this bread makes us — HAPPY.

I remember when I was a boy, we used sometimes to sing a hymn in which there were two lines, that said : —

> " Religion never was designed,
> To make our pleasures less."

Religion is intended to make us happy. And if we understand it, and make a right use of it, it will do this. Now I suppose we shall agree that David, the king of Israel, was a good judge of what will really make people happy. Sup-

pose we ask David what is the secret of true
happiness. We have his answer in the opening verses of the thirty-second Psalm. And
when we look at this Psalm we find that David
does not say: Blessed, or happy, is the man
who fights a great giant, and kills him, as I did.
He does not say : Happy is the man, who from
a poor shepherd boy rises to be the king of
a great nation, as I have done. He does not
say : Happy is the man who can write beautiful poetry, as I have done; or, Happy is the
man who sits upon a throne, and wears a crown,
as I do; or, Happy is the man who has just as
much gold and silver as he wants, as I have.
But he says : "Blessed," or happy, " is the man
whose transgression is forgiven, and whose sin
is covered." Here he teaches us that the only
real secret of true happiness, is to have our sins
pardoned. But Jesus is the only one who can
give us the pardon of our sins. And the apostle
Peter tells us that Jesus was sent into the
world on purpose to bless us, or make us
happy in just this way. In Acts iii. 26 he
says : "God sent his son to bless you, in

turning away every one of you from his in-
iquities."

And those whose sins are pardoned, and
whose hearts are changed; who are made fit for
heaven, and have a title clear to its glorious man-
sions,— are the only persons who can be truly
happy.   But this is just what Jesus does for
those who love and serve him.   And the bread
which they eat, when they believe in Jesus,
may well be called heavenly bread, because it
makes them happy.

DOING GOD'S ERRANDS.

Hester was a little girl who was trying to
love and serve Jesus.   And she showed her
love for Jesus by seeking to please him in all
that she did.   She loved to do errands for her
mother, and to have her mother say she was a
faithful servant when she did them well.

One day she had been talking with her mother about God.   As they got through, she
looked up, with a bright thought beaming in
her eyes, and said: —

" Why, mother, then God is sending us on

errands all the time! Oh! it is so nice to think that I am God's little errand girl." "Yes, dear," said her mother, "God has given us all errands to do for him, and plenty of time to do them in, and a book full of directions to show us how to do them. Every day we can tell him what we are trying to do, and ask him to help us. And when he calls us home to himself, we shall have great joy in telling him what we have been trying to do for him."

"I like that," said Hester. "It is very pleasant to be allowed to *do errands for God.*"

"One of my errands," said her mother, "is to take care of you."

"And one of mine, dear mother, is to honor and obey you. I think God gives us very pleasant errands to do."

You know that nothing makes us more happy than to do any thing for a person that we really love. This is what Jesus meant, when he said: "My yoke is easy, and my burden is light." This is what the apostle John meant when he said that — "His commandments are *not grievous.*" His people serve him from love, and this makes every thing they do for him light and pleasant to them. And here we see how eating the heavenly bread makes us happy.

THE BEST PLACE TO BEG.

Two beggars met, one day, and thus talked, as they sat together by the roadside : —

" Ours is a poor trade : I'm getting very tired of it," said one.

" Oh, are you ? " said the other. " Well, that 's not so with me. I find it a very prosperous business, and like it better every day."

" That 's strange enough ! " was the answer. " There are so many things against us. First of all, one dares not go to the same person too often."

" That 's not my experience," said the other. " I find that the oftener I go, the more readily I am heard."

" You don't say so ! " exclaimed his companion. " Why, I get turned away with ' saucy fellow,' or some such name, and am told to take myself elsewhere. As to money, or bread, I may knock pretty often before I get a bit of it."

"Now, I can truly say," said his companion, "that if I don't get just what I ask for, I always get something better instead of it."

"A lucky fellow you are; and in these times, too, when people shake their heads, and declare they need to go a begging themselves."

"Ah, I am never told that. I go where I know that riches abound, and where there is enough, and more than enough, for all that ask."

"Why," said the other, "if I put on a doleful face, they call me hypocrite; if I put on a merry air, they say I am not in want; and there's no knowing how to succeed with them."

"It's not so with me, for when I am in trouble, I get pity; and when I am full of praise and joy, I get a more abundant blessing."

"This is wonderful. I find they grow tired of my story before I am half through, and they say it is false, without caring much for me, even if it were true."

"How contrary my case is! I cannot tell my sorrows and wants too often. I am told to come with every one of them, and, strange to say, so deep is the interest in my behalf, that what I

have to tell is better known where I beg than
I know it myself."

" Why, do tell me where you beg," said the
astonished beggar.

" At the gate of heaven," said his companion.
" And where do *you* beg ? "

" Oh, *I* beg of the world," said he.

" Then no wonder you are tired of your trade.
Come and try my gate.   If you make your
stand at *that*, you will never be disappointed.
You will never get an angry or unkind word,
and never, *never* be turned empty away."   Ah!
that man had learned to eat the heavenly bread,
and you see how happy it made him.

I have only one more story to tell on this
point of our subject.   We may call it

THE INFIDEL AND THE CHRISTIAN COMPARED,
OR,
HEAR BOTH SIDES.

An infidel from London was delivering a lecture in a village in the North of England.   At
the close of his lecture, he invited any person
present, who felt disposed to do so, to ask him

any question on the subject of his lecture.   An
elderly woman, plainly dressed, rose in her
place, and said : —

"Sir, there is one question I wish to ask."

"Well, my good woman, what is it ? "

"Ten years ago," she said, "I was left a
widow with eight children, utterly unprovided
for, and nothing to call my own in the world
but my Bible.   By its help, and looking to God
for strength, I have found comfort in all my
trials, and been able to support myself and
family.   I am now tottering on the borders of
the grave ; but I am perfectly happy, because I
believe the Bible, and it teaches me to look forward to a life of immortality with Jesus in
heaven.   *This* is what *my* religion has done for
me.   Now what has *your* way of thinking done
for you ? "

"Well, my good lady," said the lecturer, " I
don't want to disturb your comfort ; but — "

" Oh, that's not the question," said the aged
woman ; "keep to the point, sir.   What has
your way of thinking done for you ? "

The infidel was unable to give any fair answer

to this question, and the meeting burst out in shouts of applause, and the enemy of the Bible had to retire from the audience, feeling that he had been fairly met and conquered by an old Christian woman.

That good woman had been eating of this heavenly bread, and, under very trying circumstances, she had found that it was able to make her happy.

And so we see that there are three reasons why Jesus may be called the heavenly bread, because, when we eat this bread, or when we love and serve him, it makes us *good*, and *great*, and *happy*.

Let us all try to love and serve Jesus, and let the prayer of our hearts to him be: "Lord, evermore give us *this bread !*"

INDEX.